Released from
Mormonism

Released from Mormonism

Living in the Truth of God's Grace

D A Hydrick

CONTENTS

INTRODUCTION

For the first fifty years of my life, I was a member of the Church of Jesus Christ of Latter-day Saints, commonly known as the Mormon Church. Before my parents joined the faith, they had three children and were content to keep it that way. As most people are aware, Mormons often have large families. My family was no exception. My parents went on to have five more children after converting to the LDS (Mormon) faith. I am child number six, so I owe my very existence to Mormonism.

Some might question why I would say anything that could undermine the LDS faith. Mormons, they would argue, are exemplary members of our society who lead good, moral lives and do much good in the world. I concur; all that is true, and I love the Mormon people.

While I struggled with my decision to write, I believe I made the right decision. I firmly believe that what I have written needs to be said. I have been open and honest in my writings. I want others to understand how I arrived at my current position, which has had such a profoundly positive impact on my life.

My motivations for sharing my story include:

Overcoming my fear. The Lord does not want us to be passive in living out the gospel (or lukewarm - Rev. 3:16). Rather, He wants us to live meaningful lives that positively impact others. The Spirit has been urging me to write about my experiences. I have a strong natural tendency to be passive, but on this matter, I cannot afford to be passive.

Gratitude. God has shown me His great love and mercy in a peculiar way. He took me through some dark and lonely times. Although the journey has not been fun, I am grateful to God every moment for the changes He has made and continues to make in me.

Desire to share the truth. The Holy Spirit teaches us truth and testifies to truth. I have discovered a tremendous, liberating freedom in truth and want others to experience it. The truth leads to a less stressful and more joy-filled life. If I do not share what I know to be the truth, I am wasting a valuable opportunity.

> Ephesians 4:15 (NASB) – *But speaking the truth in love, we are to grow up in all aspects into him, who is the head, even Christ.*

Mormons are taught to accept Jesus Christ as their personal Lord and Savior and to follow His teachings. If you define a Christian by these core beliefs, then Mormons are Christians. Beyond these core beliefs, however, Mormonism and mainstream Christianity diverge on many topics.

The Holy Spirit has led me away from Mormonism and many of the LDS faith's long-held doctrines. My prayer is to help others discover the truths and freedom I have found.

Although I have rejected many of my formerly held LDS beliefs, I do not reject any member of the LDS community. Let us discuss, share, and seek the truth together.

My intended audience includes members and potential members of the Mormon faith (specifically The Church of Jesus Christ of Latter-day Saints). If you fall into this category, I ask that you be honest with yourself and God as you read. **Consider the core beliefs that comprise your testimony.** I had a testimony as a Mormon, too, but not a testimony of certain specific doctrines unique only to Mormonism (see Chapter 11, "Spiritual Witnesses").

Those not part of my target audience can still benefit from this book. Perhaps you have friends or family members in the Mormon faith and are curious about their beliefs, or you may want to understand how Mormonism compares to mainstream Christianity.

Regardless of who you are, I hope you are a seeker of truth. I cannot ask for more than that. Please do your best to keep an open mind as you read. Be open enough to admit that you may not have all the answers. I realize this is a lot to ask because most Mormons are confident that they possess the whole truth. Seek the Holy Spirit's guidance as you read and ponder.

Chapter 1

WHAT CHANGED IN ME?

Why did I walk away from Mormonism after fifty years? The short answer is that the Holy Spirit released me from Mormonism.

Here's my story.

As a youth, I enjoyed being a member of the LDS Church (Mormon faith). I can even say that I felt the peace and love of the Holy Spirit (Holy Ghost) for the first time in an LDS church, at my baptism in Carson City, Nevada, when I was only eight. Does recognizing the Holy Spirit in an LDS church mean the church is God's official church? That's a good question, and I now believe the answer is no. I had an experience with the Spirit that day because I officially accepted Jesus Christ as my Savior.

My childhood and teenage years in South Lake Tahoe, California, were largely happy, and I had no reason to doubt the teachings I received as a member of the Mormon faith. The primary focus was on living a good, moral life and caring for those in need.

As I matured, I knew I lacked a spiritual witness of specific Mormon doctrines— a spiritual witness is defined in Mormonism as knowing something to be true through a "burning in your bosom" from the Holy Ghost — I was told that my testimony of individual LDS doctrines would develop as I served the Lord. I felt strongly enough about the LDS faith to serve as a missionary.

In 1978, at the ripe old age of nineteen, I was sent to the Arkansas Little Rock Mission. Looking back, I know that God had a plan for me—a plan initiated in the heart of the Bible Belt.

The Christians of the Deep South impressed me with their simple focus on Jesus Christ. It was refreshing. I remember thinking then – and I still believe now – that this is how it should be. The focus should always be on Christ, first and foremost.

Under Mormonism, I felt a "doctrine overload." The LDS believe in ongoing revelation, which results in the introduction of new doctrines. This additional doctrine, they would say, brings a deeper and clearer understanding. To me, the additional doctrine created complications and contradictions. I want to be clear that the LDS faith does teach Jesus Christ as our Savior, but with so many doctrines and beliefs, it is easy to lose the focus on Christ.

During my LDS mission, I served several months in the small town of Clarksdale, Mississippi. On one occasion, my missionary companion and I were invited to attend a Baptist church. I didn't expect to experience the Holy Spirit in that church, but I did. I knew God was in that church. This was confusing to me because I was taught that we Mormons had the "whole" truth. It shocked me to experience the Holy Spirit dwelling so strongly in what I had been taught was a "lesser" church (the sensation of the Holy Spirit was the same as I remembered from my baptism at age 8). Could it be that the Christian denomination you belong to does not matter as much as the simple act of accepting Jesus Christ as your savior?

I am not proud that I waited many years before admitting I felt the Spirit in that Baptist church. I succumbed to pressure.

When you are a Mormon, and especially a missionary, there is a lot of pressure to hold your ground and do the church proud. It is also a matter of family pride to serve your mission with honor.

I sorely regret holding this secret for many years. This was not the only thing I hid. Over the years, I developed many doubts about specific Mormon doctrines, but I did nothing about them. Again, I hid everything in the interest of earning acceptance from my family and church. I have sought God's forgiveness and hope He will use me to turn things around and positively impact others.

Because I harbored such doubts, I was not an "all-in" Mormon. I was sailing along, going with the flow, thinking that if I continued attending church, it would bring peace to my family. Mormons are centered firmly on family, so that was my focus—and my excuse. I was a passive man living a life of spiritual apathy. I was lukewarm at best.

> Revelation 3:15-16: *I know your deeds, that you are neither cold nor hot. I wish you were either one or the other! So, because you are lukewarm – neither hot nor cold – I am about to spit you out of my mouth.*

Unfortunately, my wife of twenty-seven years wanted a man with a strong testimony of the LDS faith. The walls came crashing down, and my wife and I divorced in 2010.

Twenty-seven years is a considerable amount of time to invest in a marriage. I still loved her and wondered if she would have me back if the Holy Ghost would help me gain a testimony of fundamental Mormon doctrine. In the back of my mind, I kept wondering if perhaps all the LDS doctrines were true and I just needed to dig deeper and pray harder to get that spiritual witness.

Others seemed to have "received a witness" that the LDS church was God's chosen church. I also wanted that testimony, not just to reconcile with my wife, but because I genuinely wanted to know the truth. I was tired of faking it.

The first few months following my divorce were incredibly lonely, and I was severely depressed. I had never lived alone. I missed my wife, kids, dog, and everything I had grown accustomed to.

God often waits until people hit rock bottom before He lifts them. That was my experience. My comfortable world ended abruptly, but that experience caused me to become humbler, dig deeper, and rely more on God. I had never prayed as much as I did in those first few months after my divorce. Unfortunately, it seemed that God was not answering me. It was not until later that I realized I was asking God the wrong questions.

Chapter 2

AND THEN IT FINALLY HAPPENED

In the summer of 2010, a lady friend and I were set to go out for dinner. A few hours before we were scheduled to meet, she called and told me she had forgotten that she had planned to attend a Joyce Meyer gathering that evening. I had no idea what she was talking about, so I asked her who Joyce Meyer was. She explained that Joyce Meyer was a well-known Christian speaker. I said, "So why don't we go together, and I'll check it out?" I am guessing that was her plan all along.

Meyer discussed something that night that grabbed my attention and changed my life. She talked about God's grace. Grace is not a common topic among Mormons.

The basic teaching was that grace is a gift from God, and Christ suffered for our sins so we might have this gift. She stated that **Grace is God's undeserved mercy toward us**, saving us from being separated from Him.

If we have faith in Jesus Christ and accept Him as our Savior, trusting in Him, His gift is mercy, which is the forgiveness of our sins through His previous suffering for our sins, leading to salvation. Meyer taught that because

1. This gift of grace and our salvation through it, we

2. naturally become filled with deep gratitude and love towards God as we accept Him, which

3. manifests itself as good works in us.

Note the order here.

As a Mormon, I was taught about grace and works in the opposite order. I was taught that if we

1. are obedient and work hard enough to do the right things (good works), then

2. after our death, God's grace will kick in and make up the difference between where we were and where we needed to be, to

3. receive salvation.

Gospel of Grace Christianity teaches that grace is a gift and the first step in the process of salvation. Mormonism teaches that grace is earned through good works and is the final step in the process of salvation (see Chapter 3, "More on Grace").

Some might argue that the Mormon view on grace appears fairer. After all, we get ahead in life through hard work and dedication. We are taught from our youth to work hard for what we want so that we will be rewarded. This is good advice, as far as earthly matters are concerned. But do we want salvation to be based on how hard we work? Think carefully about that. If God were to treat us "fairly," based on what we have "earned," we would surely all be on our way to Hell. None of us would be saved.

Romans 3:9-10 (KJV): *What then? Are we better than*

they? No, in no wise: for we have before proved both Jews and Gentiles, that they are all under sin; As it is written, **there is none righteous, no, not one**.

God has granted us His mercy through our Savior, Jesus Christ. We want mercy from God, not justice or fairness. That mercy, and our appreciation of it, will drive us to do good works—the proper, God-ordained good works as prompted by the Holy Spirit.

Good works should not be our first step in seeking God, but rather the product of our acceptance of the Savior and His acceptance of us.

1 John 5:1-3 (NIV): *Everyone who believes that Jesus is the Christ is born of God, and everyone who loves the Father loves his child as well. This is how we know that we love the children of God: by loving God and carrying out his commands. In fact, this is love for God: to keep his commands. And his commands are not burdensome.*

Note the order in these verses. First, we must love God the Father and his Son Jesus Christ. Second, we are to show our love for our fellow man by first loving God and obeying his commands. Notice how the last sentence states that "his commands are not burdensome". Why are they "not burdensome"? I believe it's because when you serve out of love, you are doing what you love. If you serve out of fear (thinking you need to earn your way to heaven), I'm confident your service will seem burdensome and stressful.

Above all else, God wants us to develop a relationship with Him. And what does He say to those who spend their lives focused on good works but fail to establish that relationship with Him?

> Matthew 7:21-23 (KJV): *Not everyone that says to me* *"Lord Lord," will enter the kingdom of heaven, but* *only the one who does the will of my Father who is in* *heaven. Many will say to me on that day "Lord Lord,* *did we not prophesy in your name and in your name* *drive out demons and in your name perform many* *miracles?" Then I will tell them plainly, "I never knew* *you. Away from me, you evildoers!"*

Joyce Meyer's version of grace resonated with me. I wondered whether God's "one true church" would teach this concept incorrectly. The LDS faith pretty much avoids the topic of grace altogether. It is rarely spoken of from the pulpit.

Upon returning home from the Joyce Meyer event, I found many new concepts troubling me. In my confusion, I decided again to read from the Book of Mormon and pray for a spiritual witness of its truthfulness. I was genuinely conflicted. On the one hand, I still wanted that testimony regarding Mormonism so I could get back on track with my former life. But, on the other hand, my new learning was moving me in the opposite direction. I was growing more desperate for the truth.

I prayed again for a spiritual witness of the truthfulness of the Book of Mormon, as I had done many times before, with no response. After praying, as I sat and quietly pondered my situation, I asked God, "Should I walk away from Mormonism?" Finally, I had asked the right question.

Immediately upon saying those words, I felt the Holy Spirit begin to enter me. The sensation started at the top of my head and gradually spread down through my body to my hands and feet. The Holy Spirit was letting me know that God heard my prayer, and it was time to walk away without question.

The sensation of the Holy Spirit was a pleasant tingling current that grew slowly in intensity. This calming manifestation was accompanied by a sense of joy and freedom, as well as a profound feeling of gratitude and relief. I had never experienced the Holy Spirit in this manner nor so strongly.

I realized that I had just been liberated. I sat on the couch for several minutes with a huge smile on my face, knowing God had finally answered my prayers. At that moment, He released me from my many years of struggles in searching for an LDS testimony. It was not the answer I had expected, but I knew it was from God. The amount of gratitude and joy I felt was overwhelming.

Living as a Mormon carries a lot of pressure. It is a faith of works with little tolerance for imperfection. But the weight of all that expectation went away that night. "Liberated" is not a strong enough word to explain what God did for me, and I have been living in joy ever since.

The way I see it, God probably got tired of me repeatedly asking the same wrong questions (I was still expecting an answer to affirm Mormonism as God's church). It was as if God finally said, "Enough!" and met me where I was, ending it.

Jesus's words, "the truth will make you free" (John 8:32 KJV), had real meaning to me that night. The truth frees you from the bondage of incorrect doctrine. God removes all the extra "stuff" that bogs you down, and you realize that the truth is pure and simple. The truth is that God wants us to know Him, to be in relationship with Him, and to live in gratitude to Him.

This is my personal experience and testimony, and, to me, it is very real. This experience will stay with me and impact me for the rest of my life. It pushes me forward with boldness and confidence in the face of negative consequences. It is the catalyst that accelerated my learning and started me on an incredible journey. I have faith that the journey will continue.

I will share what I have "uncovered" since that special night in the remaining chapters. Although I could go into many details, I want to focus on what has struck me the deepest—the truth that the Spirit opened my eyes to.

Chapter 3

MORE ON GRACE

Many who read this will try to refute what I wrote in the previous chapter regarding the Mormon teaching on grace. This chapter should help clarify how the grace defined by Mormonism differs from the grace I now accept in the context of "Gospel of Grace Christianity". Grace was rarely a topic of discussion in my LDS experience, but lately, grace hasn't been buried as deeply. This change may be related to the church's push for acceptance among Christians with their "We are Christians too" campaign, which was initiated by LDS president Gordon B. Hinckley around 2007.

One example of this LDS movement towards acceptance by other Christians is the 2024 addition of several well-known Christian hymns to the LDS hymnal, including "Amazing Grace." I am mixed about this. Amazing Grace is a fantastic song with truthful lyrics; however, I question the church's motives behind including it in the LDS hymnal.

As noted in the previous chapter, I have found that the LDS definition of grace differs from the mainstream Christian definition. LDS doctrine emphasizes works and righteousness as requirements for salvation. Consider the following statement by Bruce R. McConkie in his book Mormon Doctrine:

> *Grace is granted to men proportionately as they conform to the standards of personal righteousness that are part of the gospel plan.*

This statement certainly leads one to believe that grace is given out bit by bit only as we are righteous enough to receive it. By this definition, grace is not a gift but a reward; something we must earn.

Consider also the following from the Dictionary of the LDS version of the King James Bible:

> *This grace is an enabling power that allows men and women to lay hold on eternal life and exaltation **after they have expended their own best efforts**. Divine grace is needed by every soul in consequence of the fall of Adam and also because of man's weaknesses and shortcomings. However, **grace cannot suffice without total effort on the part of the recipient**. Hence the explanation, "It is by grace that we are saved, **after all we can do**." (Book of Mormon 2 Nephi 25:23)*

From these writings (and there are many others), we see that Mormon doctrine teaches that we are indeed saved by grace (biblical), but only if we work hard enough to become worthy of that grace (not biblical). Here is a final example from the Articles of Faith authored by the LDS Prophet Joseph Smith and accepted as Mormon scripture:

Article of Faith #3
*We believe that through the Atonement of Christ, all mankind may be **saved by obedience** to the laws and ordinances of the Gospel.*

Here we are told that we are saved by "obedience" (and I think it is safe to say that "obedience" is another word for "works" and is not a synonym for "grace").

Does obedience save us? Obedience is undoubtedly important, but let's consider what the Bible says about how we gain salvation. **The Bible clearly states that grace is a gift received by faith and does not come through our works.**

Ephesians 2:8-9 (NIV): *For it is by grace you have been saved, through faith – and this is not from yourselves, it is the gift of God – not by works, so that no one can boast.*

I am convinced that the word "faith", as used in verse 8, means more than simply believing in Jesus Christ. This faith is a trust and reliance on God. We trust God to the point that we surrender to him and are moved to repentance.

Good works are important, and we are blessed for them (both on earth and in heaven), but works are not a requirement for salvation, and our works do not make God love us more. He already loves us completely.

I have heard "good works" defined as the outcome of our faith. They are the fruit or evidence of transformation to a new life in Christ. Good works demonstrate how much we love God and appreciate his sacrifice. We do good works naturally as an expression of genuine gratitude to God.

I was fortunate to come across a well-written manual on grace titled "Grace Immersion." It was written by Pastor Rene

Schlaepfer, the Pastor of Twin Lakes Church in Aptos, California (www.graceimmersion.com).[1]

As a Christian newcomer, I found *Grace Immersion* to be an excellent tool that God used to help me understand His grace. I recommend it to everyone. I have reread it several times because its message is essential for all of us to understand. Many thanks to Pastor Rene and especially his wife, Laurie, who helped me transition from Mormonism to "gospel of grace Christianity." Laurie was also a great help to me in writing this book. I am eternally grateful.

Rene states in *Grace Immersion* that *"we experience abundant joy and freedom when we understand the concept of* grace". I know this to be true because that is precisely what I experienced on that special night, and I am happy to report that the joy and freedom continue.

The word "legalism" is frequently referenced in Christianity. As a Mormon, I had never encountered the concept of legalism. The word does not appear in the bible. So, what does legalism mean to a Christian? The Pharisees serve as notable examples of legalistic individuals. They added additional, very granular and demanding rules to the Jewish law that are not found in Scripture (many of these rules were based on tradition – see Matthew 15:1-3). This is one reason Christ had so many issues with the Pharisees: He came to bring grace, but they were primarily focused on the details of the law.

One could say that legalism is the opposite of grace. A legalistic approach to God is performance-oriented and rule-driven, while a grace-oriented approach is based on our relationship with God and others. Here are some comparisons between performance-oriented religion and grace-oriented faith from Rene's book:

Performance-oriented: I obey; therefore, I am accepted.

The gospel of grace: I am accepted; therefore, I obey.

Performance-oriented: My self-worth is based mainly on how hard I work or how moral I am, and I find myself looking down on the lazy or immoral.

The gospel of grace: My self-image is centered on the One who died for me. I am a sinner saved by sheer grace, so how could I look down on anyone?

Another thought from *Grace Immersion* is that both sin and legalism make us slaves. We are slaves to whatever controls us. I can testify that there is no freedom in legalism. It is very confining. When the Holy Spirit directed me to leave Mormonism, I immediately felt the joyous freedom that comes from God's grace. I have never been happier.

You might ask, "Does the freedom gained through saving grace mean we can do whatever we want without worry of losing our salvation?" This is not a new question.

Romans 6:15 (KJV): *"Shall we sin because we are not under the law but under grace? By no means!"*

1 Peter 2:16 (NLT): *"You are free ... but don't use your freedom as an excuse to do evil."*

In my LDS experience, the overwhelming feeling that Mormons had towards the "Saved by Grace" Christians was that they erred in their belief because it simply made no sense that someone could accept God and then live in whatever way they liked (and yet still be worthy of salvation).

The Bible teaches us that our actions express our level of faith, which is characterized by our trust and surrender to God and His will. If we are truly converted and accept Christ as our savior, we will do good, not evil. Our lives will mirror our faith.

Francis Chan was a speaker at the church I attended in the Sacramento area. I appreciate how he expressed the truth about surrendering to God and how this surrendering affects our lives. He said that as we surrender, we "become a new person and hunger and thirst for what is right."

> John 14:12: *I tell you the truth, anyone who believes in me will do the same works I have done...*

What was my experience in the Mormon "legalistic" culture? I certainly had a very different experience as a Mormon from what I have had as a gospel of grace Christian. As a Mormon, life was performance-driven. I was taught that if I worked hard enough and stayed righteous, I would earn a spot in the Celestial Kingdom (the highest heaven in Mormon belief – see Chapter 8, "The LDS Plan of Salvation"). **My obedience to God was stressed far above my relationship with God.**

As a gospel of grace Christian, I understand that I cannot do life on my own. My effort will never be enough to earn a spot in heaven.

Making the move out of legalism has not been easy. I fight it every day. Undoing a lifetime of incorrect thinking can be a challenging task.

Legalism has even affected my personality and my mental health. I am very rule-driven and am not as open as I should be. In other words, I am not as free as I should be. This is because I have a long-held need to appear in control and without weakness. I know this facade is wrong, yet I fight a constant personal battle with it.

I can see how this problem stems mainly from the Mormon teaching that perfection is an attainable goal. Feeling the need to live a perfect life (or nearly perfect life) or potentially lose your salvation can cause tremendous stress.

The LDS understand the verse "be ye therefore perfect" (Matt. 5:48 KJV) as a command to become perfect through our own human efforts. That is an impossibility. Jesus Christ is the only perfect one. It is only through Christ that we can be made perfect.

> Hebrews 10:14 (NIV): *For by one sacrifice he has made perfect forever those who are being made holy.*

Chapter 4

THE BIBLE

In The Articles of *Faith* by Joseph Smith, we read:

Article of Faith #8
*We believe the Bible to be the word of God **as far as it is translated correctly**; we also believe the Book of Mormon to be the word of God.*

The Mormon teaching is that the Book of Mormon is entirely accurate, being the word of God, whereas the Bible has translation issues. The Bible is only true "as far as it is translated correctly." In other words, the Bible is not as pure or complete as other LDS scriptures. The Bible has been tainted.

Joseph Smith also wrote (*The Teachings of Joseph Smith*, page 327):

I believe the Bible as it read when it came from the pen of the original writers, ignorant translators, careless transcribers, or designing and corrupt priests have committed many errors.

In my experience, Mormons focused more intently on the Book of Mormon and other LDS scriptures than on the Bible. This is a sad reality.

Author Philip Barlow wrote an article entitled "Future of Mormonism—Mormons and the Bible in the 21st Century."[2] In this article, he argues that the Book of Mormon is the primary focus of the LDS faith.

> *... Deriving from the church presidency of Ezra Taft Benson (1985-1994), a renewed and heightened emphasis on the Book of Mormon has meant that it has taken a certain priority over the Bible in Mormon culture and consciousness -at least in the form of Mormonism embodied in The Church of Jesus Christ of Latter-day Saints, whose headquarters are in Salt Lake City. ...*

> *The new emphasis on the Book of Mormon in the dominant LDS Church could be overstated, for the Bible remains an essential component of official and popular perspectives and study. Nonetheless, when one visits a typical Mormon worship service today, one will hear church members cite and bear witness to the inspired nature of the Book of Mormon more frequently than they cite or testify of the Bible. It remains to be seen whether this will invite an eventual corrective, but the trend has considerable momentum with no hint of an end in sight.*

Christians take offense when they hear the Bible referred to as containing doctrinal errors (or even missing doctrine). The

Bible is sacred and is the standard for all Christians.

My common sense and logic tell me that God would not provide us with a flawed Bible, and experts in the field will also confirm that God has preserved the Bible. There are no significant doctrinal issues.

In his book, Seven Reasons Why You Can Trust the Bible, Dr. Erwin W. Lutzer presents numerous compelling arguments that demonstrate the Bible's authenticity. One of those arguments pertains to the Dead Sea Scrolls. He wrote:

> *These scrolls are some eight hundred to a thousand years older than other previously known manuscripts. Portions of every book of the Old Testament have been found except for Esther... Most important was a complete scroll of the book of Isaiah... Dr. Gleason L. Archer observes that the two **copies of Isaiah found in the caves proved to be word for word identical with our standard Hebrew Bible in more than 95% of the text**. The 5% variation consisted chiefly of obvious slips of the pen and variations in spelling.*[3]

This is firm evidence that what we have in the Bible, specifically the Old Testament, is what God intended us to have. There is no significant loss of content or major issues with translation. The Bible is the inspired Word of God—period. It is God's blueprint for us, guiding us toward happy lives and, more importantly, eternal happiness.

Other evidence supporting the authenticity of the Bible includes prophecies that have been fulfilled and historical evidence for the people and events detailed in the Bible. The following is from the Institute for Creation Research.[4]

The Bible has become a significant source book for secular archaeology, helping to identify such ancient figures as Sargon (Isaiah 20:1); Sennacherib (Isaiah 37:37); Horam of Gazer (Joshua 10:33); Hazar (Joshua 15:27); and the nation of the Hittites (Genesis 15:20). The biblical record, unlike other 'scriptures,' is historically set, opening itself up for testing and verification.

Two of the greatest 20th-century archaeologists, William F. Albright and Nelson Glueck, both lauded the Bible (even though they were non-Christian and secular in their training and personal beliefs) as being the single most accurate source document from history. Over and over again, the Bible has been found to be accurate in its places, dates, and records of events. No other 'religious' document comes even close.

The 19th-century critics used to deny the historicity of the Hittites, the Horites, the Edomites, and various other peoples, nations, and cities mentioned in the Bible. Those critics have long been silenced by the archaeologist's spade, and few critics dare to question the geographical and ethnological reliability of the Bible.

The names of over 40 different kings of various countries mentioned in the Bible have all been found in contemporary documents and inscriptions outside of the Old Testament, and are always consistent *with the times and places associated with them in the Bible. **Nothing exists in ancient literature that has been even remotely as well-confirmed in accuracy as has the Bible**.*

Taking the stance that the Bible has errors gives the Mormon faith license to change the parts of the Bible that conflict with their doctrine (and to add additional doctrine as they see fit). To me, this seems awfully convenient—and awfully dangerous.

Joseph Smith adopted this position from the early days of Mormonism, revising portions of the Bible in what is known as "The Inspired Version", also called the JST (Joseph Smith Translation). Today, the King James Version is the accepted version of the Bible used in the LDS Church. Still, the official church copies contain many footnotes that show the Joseph Smith translations of verses he believed to be "mistranslated."

Through the JST, Joseph Smith also wrote himself and references to the Book of Mormon into the Bible (specifically at the end of the book of Genesis):

JST Genesis 50:30-33:

And again, a seer will I raise up out of the fruit of thy loins, and unto him will I give power to bring forth my word unto the seed of thy loins; and not to the bringing forth of my word only, saith the Lord, but to the convincing them of my word, which shall have already gone forth among them in the last days; Wherefore the fruit of thy loins shall write, and the fruit of the loins of Judah shall write; and that which shall be written by the fruit of thy loins, and also that which shall be written by the fruit of the loins of Judah, shall grow together unto the confounding of false doctrines, and laying down of contentions, and establishing peace among the fruit of thy loins, and bringing them to a knowledge of their fathers in the latter days; and also to the knowledge of my covenants, saith the Lord. And out of weakness shall he be made strong, in that day when my work shall go forth among all my people, which shall restore them, who are of the house of Israel, in the last days. And that seer will I bless, and they that seek to destroy him shall be confounded; for this promise I give unto you; for I will remember you from generation to generation; and his name shall be called Joseph, and it shall be after the name of his father; and he shall be like unto you; for the thing which the Lord shall bring forth by his hand shall bring my people unto salvation.

Joseph Smith's father was also named Joseph. It seems odd, and even arrogant, that Joseph Smith added himself to the sacred words of the Bible. It does not sit right with me, and I believe that is because the Holy Spirit is telling me it is not right.

John Divito of Mormonism Research Ministry wrote the following:

No evidence exists that this text was originally included in the biblical book of Genesis. Not a single Hebrew document exists to support Smith's alteration of the Book of Genesis. It seems that beginning with verse 24, Joseph Smith inserted his own text.

Chapter 5

THE BOOK OF MORMON AND OTHER LDS SCRIPTURE

The eighth Article of Faith, previously quoted, not only states that the Bible is true "as far as it is translated correctly," but also states that the Book of Mormon "is" the word of God. In the introduction to the Book of Mormon, Joseph Smith wrote:

> *I told the brethren that the Book of Mormon was the most correct of any book on earth, and the keystone of our religion, and a man would get nearer to God by abiding by its precepts, than by any other book.* [5]

The Book of Mormon is one of four books of scripture in the LDS canon. The other three are the Bible, the Doctrine and Covenants, and the Pearl of Great Price. The Book of Mormon was written as an account of the ancient inhabitants of America and includes their history. It teaches that a small group of Israelites, also known as Jews, left Jerusalem around 600 BC and migrated to the Americas. Over approximately 1,000 years, these people divided into two groups: the righteous Nephites and the unrighteous Lamanites, who went to war against one another. The Book of Mormon also contains the religious history of these people and an account of Christ's visit to them after His resurrection.

In my youth, the LDS teaching was that "all" Native Americans are descendants of this original Israelite group (specifically the Lamanites). Spencer W. Kimball, a former LDS Prophet, said the following at a Lamanite Youth Conference in April 1971:

> *With pride I tell those who come to my office that a Lamanite is a descendant of one Lehi who left Jerusalem six hundred years before Christ and with his family crossed the mighty deep and landed in America. And Lehi and his family* ***became the ancestors of "all" of the Indian and Mestizo tribes in North and South and Central America and in the islands of the sea.***

In 1981, an introductory paragraph was added to the Book of Mormon, which stated in part:

After thousands of years, all were destroyed except the Lamanites, and ***they are the "principal" ancestors of the American Indians.***

Starting in the 1990s, however, DNA evidence came forward that contradicted the teaching that Native Americans are of Jewish or Semitic origin. This science concluded that the ancestors of Native American peoples ***migrated from Asia.*** [6]

Before the DNA evidence surfaced, the LDS church was still teaching that Native Americans were descendants of these Israelites (of Lamanite extraction). After the DNA evidence called into question the LDS teaching that Native Americans are descendants of Israelites, the 2006 edition of the Book of Mormon had a wording change in the introduction. It now states that:

> *the Lamanites...* "are among" the ancestors of the American Indians.

Over the years, the church's teaching regarding the ancestry of Native Americans has continued to change. First, an LDS prophet stated that "all" Native Americans were of Jewish descent. Next, the church taught that the "principal ancestors" of the Native Americans were of Jewish descent. The church is now stating that Semitic DNA is "among" the American Indians. Good science was used to challenge and correct false teachings within the church.

A *USA Today* article titled "DNA research and Mormon scholars changing basic beliefs" stated the following:

> *Plant geneticist Simon Southerton was a Mormon bishop in Brisbane, Australia when he woke up the morning of Aug. 3, 1998 to the shattering conclusion that his knowledge of science made it impossible for him to believe any longer in the Book of Mormon.*

> *Two years later he started writing "Losing a Lost Tribe: Native Americans, DNA and the Mormon Church," published by Signature Books... Along the way, he found a world of scholarship that has led him to conclude The Church of Jesus Christ of*

Latter-day Saints belief is changing, but not through prophesy and revelation. Rather, Southerton sees a behind-the-scenes revolution led by a small group of Brigham Young University scholars and their critics who are reinterpreting fundamental teachings of the Book of Mormon in light of DNA research findings. Along the way, he says, these apologist scholars, with the apparent blessing of church leadership, are contradicting church teachings about the origins of American Indians and Polynesians.

"You've got Mormon apologists in their own publications rejecting what prophets have been saying for decades," Southerton said.

And while the work of the BYU apologists — the term means those who speak or write in defense of something — remains confined largely to intellectual circles, some church members who have always understood themselves in light of Mormon teachings about the people known as Lamanites are suffering identity crises.

"It's very difficult. It is almost traumatizing," said Jose Aloayza, a Midvale attorney who likened facing this new reality to staring into a spiritual abyss.

"It's that serious, that real," said Aloayza, a Peruvian native born into the church and still a member. "I'm almost here feeling I need an apology. Our prophets should have known better. That's the feeling I get."

> *Southerton, now a senior researcher with the Commonwealth Scientific and Industrial Research Organization in Canberra, Australia, has concluded along with many other scientists studying mitochondrial DNA lines that* **American Indians and Polynesians are of Asian extraction**.[6]

For years, I was taught that the Israelite people of the Book of Mormon settled in the region around Central America. In the 1960s, 70s, and 80s, you could book guided tours in Central America that claimed to show you the ancient ruins of these Israelite people. Some of my family members and friends went on these tours. In more recent years, the LDS view has flipped, and the current claim is that these Israelites lived in the Great Lakes region of the United States.

Some recent DNA evidence has been uncovered showing traces of Jewish DNA among small groups of Native Americans. I found the following in The Jerusalem Post, *Exploring the connections between Jews and Native Americans*, by Walter Bingham (July 2, 2021):

> *According to a Ynet report, a population of Native American Indians from the US state of Colorado has been found to have a genetic mutation typical of Ashkenazi Jews. The finding suggests the presence of common roots that date back to the days of Christopher Columbus.*

This Jewish DNA, however, emerged in America long after the timeframe of the Book of Mormon. The Book of Mormon time-line ends more than a thousand years before Columbus arrived in America.

Mormon apologists also claim that some Jewish DNA was recently found in tribes in the Midwestern United States. This does not support the church's earlier teachings, however, that most Native Americans descended from the Lamanites. It appears there is some desperate grasping at straws here in an attempt to find evidence for the Book of Mormon.

The Bible in the Book of Mormon

In my studies of the New Testament, I began to notice certain stories that seemed remarkably similar to those found in the Book of Mormon. Not only are many stories similar, but specific verses are very similar.

One night during my Bible study, I read a verse that caught my full attention – not because of the meaning of the scripture but because I knew I had read it, or something very similar to it, in the Book of Mormon. The scripture was John 11:50, which reads:

> *Nor consider that it is expedient for us, that one man should die for the people, and that the whole nation perish not.*

Now compare this verse to 1 Nephi 4:13 in the Book of Mormon:

> *Behold the Lord slayeth the wicked to bring forth his righteous purposes. It is better that one man should perish than that a nation should dwindle and perish in unbelief.*

These verses are very similar (too similar to be a coincidence). The words in John 11:50 are the politically motivated words of Caiaphas, the high priest, suggesting that killing Jesus is a necessary step in avoiding Roman retaliation. The irony here is that his words ultimately became a prophetic statement about the atoning sacrifice of Jesus Christ.

The words in 1 Nephi 4:13 come from the story of Nephi being justified by the Holy Spirit in the murder of Laban, a man who had possession of brass plates containing scripture. It is stated that these plates were necessary in preserving the gospel message for those about to travel to the Americas.

The account of Nephi killing Laban is dated to approximately 600 years before the birth of Christ. If these Book of Mormon verses were true, the words of Caiaphas would be a repeat of Nephi's words more than 600 years earlier. For me, this is too much to believe.

There are more examples of out-of-sequence verses from the Bible that are essentially repeated in The Book of Mormon. These are known as "anachronistic" verses. We see another good example in comparing Malachi 4:1 to 1 Nephi 22:15.

Malachi 4:1 (KJV): For, behold, the day cometh, that shall burn as an oven; and all the proud, yea, and all that do wickedly, shall be stubble: and the day that cometh shall burn them up, saith the Lord of hosts, that it shall leave them neither root nor branch.

1 Nephi 22:15: For behold, saith the prophet, the time cometh speedily that Satan shall have no more power over the hearts of the children of men; for the day soon cometh that all the proud and they who do wickedly shall be as stubble; and the day cometh that they must be burned.

The problem here is that the people of the Book of Mormon are recorded as having left Jerusalem before the Babylonian captivity. Malachi was a prophet after the Babylonian captivity. How could his words appear in a Book of Mormon passage from years earlier?

One of my earliest doubts about the Book of Mormon arose one evening when I read 2 Nephi 25:19, which is dated to the period between 559 and 545 BC in the Book of Mormon. (approximately 550 years before Christ).

> *For according to the words of the prophets, the Messiah cometh in six hundred years from the time that my father left Jerusalem; and according to the words of the prophets, and also the word of the angel of God, his name shall be Jesus Christ, the Son of God.*

This verse states that the name of the Messiah shall be Jesus Christ. When I read this, I immediately sensed that I was not reading ancient scripture from hundreds of years before Christ. It struck me that this was likely modern writing. Nowhere in the Old Testament is the name Jesus Christ found. The Messiah of the Old Testament had many titles, but Jesus Christ was not one of them. Are we to believe that the Israelites of the Book of Mormon knew the Messiah's earthly title of Jesus Christ, hundreds of years before he was born?

I am not the only person who has noticed similarities between the Bible and the Book of Mormon. You can find comparisons all over the Internet.

Here is an example I found which compares the Sermon on the Mount version in Matthew 5-7 (KJV) with the sermon recorded in the Book of Mormon in 3rd Nephi 12-14:

- <u>Matthew 5 vs 3 Nephi 12</u>

  *326 words (31%) of the original 1049 words of Matthew 5 were deleted and 358 new words (33%) were added to the text to create 3 Nephi 12 which has a total of 1081 words, of which **66% are verbatim**, copied from Matthew 5.*

- <u>Matthew 6 vs 3 Nephi 13</u>

  *43 words (5%) of the original 788 words of Matthew 6 were deleted and 86 new words (10%) were added to the text to create 3 Nephi 13 which has a total of 831 words, of which **90% are verbatim**, copied from Matthew 6.*

- <u>Matthew 7 vs 3 Nephi 14</u>

  *13 words (2%) of the original 594 words of Matthew 7 were deleted and 37 new words (6%) were added to the text to create 3 Nephi 14 which has a total of 631 words, of which **94% are verbatim** copied from Matthew 7.*

- <u>Aggregate Matthew 5-7 vs 3 Nephi 12-14</u>

  *382 words (16%) of the original 2431 words of Matthew 5-7 were deleted and 481 new words (19%) were added to the text to create 3 Nephi 12-14 which has a total of 2543 words, of which **81% are verbatim** copied from Matthew 5-7* [7]

Considering the entire sermon, approximately 80% of the words are identical. This makes it extremely difficult for me to believe anything other than the obvious. These verses were copied from the King James Version of the Bible.

It appears that Joseph Smith used the King James Version of the Bible as a source in writing the Book of Mormon. The overwhelming evidence makes it difficult to believe that the origin of the Book of Mormon is as Joseph Smith claimed. From a scientific view, most Native Americans are of Asian origin and are not descendants of the Israelites (of Semitic origin). There is also considerable evidence demonstrating that parts of the Book of Mormon were copied from the King James Version of the Bible.

Laying aside the evidence for the moment and simply focusing on my own experience with the Holy Spirit, I share this. I was praying to know the truth of the Book of Mormon when the Holy Spirit directed me to walk away from Mormonism. For many years, I had prayed earnestly to know the truth of the Book of Mormon, but I received no spiritual witness.

Others claim to have had a spiritual witness of the Book of Mormon. It is not my intent to call anyone a liar; I simply attest that I never had that experience.

The Pearl of Great Price

The "Standard Works" (canonized scripture) in the LDS faith include the Bible, the Book of Mormon, the Doctrine and Covenants, and the Pearl of Great Price. *The Pearl of Great Price* is the shortest of the Standard Works and contains a section titled "The Book of Abraham." This book has aroused serious controversy.

Joseph Smith claimed to have translated "The Book of Abraham" from a portion of some papyrus scrolls. The scrolls were written in Egyptian, and Joseph Smith purported that parts of these scrolls were written by Abraham himself, "by his own hand." The scrolls, along with some Egyptian mummies, were delivered to Smith by Michael Chandler in 1835. Smith purchased the entire collection for $2,400.00.

Along with the scroll translations, the Book of Abraham also contains illustrations (replicating the original papyrus's drawings). Joseph Smith hired a wood carver to create the illustrations.

Joseph Smith's mother, Lucy Mack Smith, kept the mummies and papyrus collection for several years after Joseph's death. Emma Smith eventually sold the collection to Abel Combs, who split the collection up (according to a Brigham Young University paper titled "A History of the Joseph Smith Papyri and Book of Abraham").[8] Part of the collection was sold to the St. Louis Museum, which in turn was sold to the Wood Museum. The Wood Museum, which had relocated to Chicago, was destroyed in the Great Chicago Fire of 1871.

The remaining portion of the collection was acquired by the New York Metropolitan Museum in 1947. In 1967, the museum donated the papyri to the LDS Church after receiving a gift from an anonymous donor. John Gee, the author of the BYU paper mentioned above, stated: "I conservatively estimate that the remaining papyrus fragments amount to at most thirteen percent of what Joseph Smith once had."

What did the remaining papyrus contain? The papyrus had the same images as the illustrations in the Book of Abraham, further demonstrating their authenticity.

During Joseph Smith's lifetime, ancient Egyptian was a language of mystery. Nobody knew how to read it. This is not the case today. The fragments of the remaining scrolls have been translated yet again. This time, the translators (both LDS and non-LDS Egyptologists) claim the fragments have nothing to do with Abraham but are instead parts of "The Book of the Dead," an ancient funerary text. Furthermore, the fragments date to approximately the first century BC, at least 1,700 years after Abraham is believed to have lived.

Are we to believe that Abraham wrote some of the missing fragments from the collection? That is a lot to ask someone to buy into. What are the odds that Joseph Smith's randomly purchased Egyptian mummy collection also included scrolls with Abraham's writings? The story is improbable and too unbelievable to be true.

For those who wish to examine the evidence for themselves, there is a massive volume of data on the Internet, including explanations from LDS apologists. To date, I have not read an explanation from the LDS viewpoint that satisfies me. I encourage all to research the issue and weigh the evidence for themselves.

The Pearl of Great Price contains another small book titled "The Book of Moses," which is a revision of the biblical book of Genesis. Joseph Smith wrote the Book of Moses between June 1830 and February 1831 (originally as the beginning of the Joseph Smith Translation of the Bible). It was published as part of t*he Pearl of Great Price* in 1851.

The books of Abraham and Moses contain direct contradictions to one another in the creation narratives. When comparing Moses 2 with Abraham 4, we find the following:

> *Moses 2: ...The Lord spake unto Moses, saying:... yea, in the beginning I created the heaven and the earth upon which thou standest... And I, God, said: Let there be light, and there was light.*

Abraham 4: And then the Lord said: Let us go down. And they went down at the beginning, and they, that is the Gods, organized and formed the heavens and the earth… And they (the Gods) said: Let there be light; and there was light.

Was God the creator, or was He simply one of "the gods" involved in creation? Did Abraham and Moses contradict each other, or did Joseph Smith contradict himself in his writings? What does the Bible teach about the creation of the earth?

Isaiah 44:24 (NIV): *This is what the LORD says – your Redeemer, who formed you in the womb: I am the LORD, the Maker of all things, who stretches out the heavens, **who spreads out the earth by myself**.*

When you compare the time frames of the Moses and Abraham verses above, it becomes even more interesting. The Book of Moses was written between 1830 and 1831, much earlier than the Book of Abraham's Section 4, which was written between 1835 and 1842. The doctrines recorded by Joseph Smith seem to have evolved over this time frame from a monotheistic doctrine of one god to a polytheistic doctrine of a plurality of gods. We will observe a pattern of doctrinal evolution repeating itself as we proceed.

Chapter 6

CONTRADICTIONS BETWEEN THE BIBLE AND LDS SCRIPTURE

In my later days as a Mormon, I conducted a small experiment. I would alternate between reading from the Bible and the Book of Mormon. I soon noticed I was looking forward to my Bible studies. I experienced the peace of the Holy Spirit when reading from the Bible, especially the New Testament. Still, I never experienced the Holy Spirit when reading from the Book of Mormon.

As I studied the New Testament, I discovered differences between what the Bible says and what Mormon doctrine teaches. This was a sign that many of my doubts regarding Mormon doctrine might have merit.

I have labeled some LDS doctrine as "warm and fuzzy." The doctrine sounds great, and I wish it were true, but it is not biblical. Let's examine some doctrinal discrepancies between the Bible and LDS doctrine.

"The Great Apostasy"

LDS doctrine states that the priesthood was taken from the earth as the apostles of old were slain. As a result, the "true church" was believed to have been removed from the Earth. This removal of God's church is known to Mormons as "the Great Apostasy" (which lasted about 1,700 years). The doctrine also states that Joseph Smith was used "as an instrument of God" to restore the gospel in 1830 (in restoring the gospel, the priesthood was taught to have been restored as well).

The belief in a Great Apostasy is not exclusive to Mormonism. During the "Second Great Awakening" of the late 18th and early 19th centuries, many Protestant groups came to believe that a restoration of the gospel was necessary. Restorationist denominations that emerged from this movement include the Swedenborgians, the Mormons, and the Seventh-day Adventists, among others. They held that traditional Christianity had fallen into error and thus, the true faith needed to be restored.

The LDS Great Apostasy teaching does not resonate with me. Jesus promised to send the Holy Spirit after His departure. Would the Lord give us the wonderful gift of the Holy Spirit only to turn around and remove His church from the earth shortly thereafter? That does not make sense.

The following verses also indicate that God would not allow this apostasy to occur:

> *Matthew 28:20 (NIV): ...And surely I am with you always, to the very end of the age.*

> *Matthew 16:18 (KJV): ...Upon this rock I will build my church **and the gates of hell shall not prevail against it**.*

The "gates of hell" (gates of Hades) is a metaphor for death (Job 17:16; 38:17; Psalm 9:13; 107:18). The meaning of Matthew 16:18, therefore, is that death would not prevail against or overcome the church.

Yes, the early church went through many trials and growing pains. For example, heresy had to be dealt with by the leaders in the early church, but did God eradicate His church from the earth? He promised He would not do so, and I believe God's promises. In my opinion, to say that the church of Christ was removed entirely from the earth would mean that the "gates of hell" did indeed "prevail against it."

I don't want to be too simplistic regarding the topic of apostasy. The Bible indicates that apostasy will occur during the end times, but it does not state that the church itself will be removed from the earth. I believe that the apostasy referred to in the Bible is personal apostasy, and not the death of the church itself.

> *Matthew 24:10-13 (ESV): And then many will fall away and betray one another and hate one another. And many false prophets will arise and lead many astray. And because lawlessness will be increased, the love of many will grow cold.* ***But the one who endures to the end will be saved***.

Eternal Marriage

This is one of the warm and fuzzy Mormon doctrines I mentioned earlier. The LDS church teaches that marriage is not only for this life but can be for all eternity as well (the doctrine goes on to include the possibility of our families being eternal family units). I believe we will undoubtedly have close relationships with those we love in this life in the life to come, but the Bible does not teach a doctrine of eternal marriage or eternal families. Consider the words of the Savior Himself:

> *Luke 20:34-35 (NIV): ...The people of this age marry and are given in marriage, but those who are considered worthy of taking part in the age to come and in the resurrection from the dead will neither marry nor be given in marriage.*

As a Mormon, I was taught that these verses of scripture prove only that we need to be married, or "sealed for time and all eternity," while living on this earth, because there will be no marriage ceremonies after this life in heaven. I think this interpretation is a stretch. The scripture seems to indicate that there is no marriage in heaven.

Another Mormon doctrine holds that you cannot attain the highest degree of Heaven (Exaltation in the Celestial Kingdom – see Chapter 8, "The LDS Plan of Salvation") unless you are married for eternity by those in authority to seal you as husband and wife. Marriage is therefore strongly encouraged.

What did the Apostle Paul say about marriage? Quite a lot. Here is one of his teachings:

> *1 Corinthians 7:8-9 (RSV): To the unmarried and the widows I say that it is well for them to remain single as I do. But if they cannot exercise self-control, they should marry. For it is better to marry than to be aflame with passion.*

This is hardly a ringing endorsement of marriage. This passage implies that marriage is for the weak.

Please understand me. I realize that God ordains marriage, but I am not familiar with a single verse in the Bible that refers to marriage as an eternal husband-wife relationship. I am sure we form eternal bonds with those we have had a relationship with here on earth, but marriage is not a heavenly institution.

Where did the concept of eternal marriage come from? I researched the topic and found that as early as 1749, a man named Emanuel Swedenborg wrote about eternal marriage. Swedenborg was a Swedish mystic who claimed the Savior visited him when he was fifty-seven. There are notable similarities between the stories and teachings of Swedenborg and Joseph Smith (see http://craigwmiller.tripod.com/interest.htm for more on Swedenborg).

Joseph Smith married Sarah Cleveland, whose husband, John, was a Swedenborgian at the time of her plural marriage to Joseph in 1842. In July 1843, Joseph Smith wrote his revelation regarding eternal marriage in Section 132 of the Doctrine and Covenants.

What did Swedenborg teach? He taught that there are three heavens, with the celestial heaven being the most refined. You must have an eternal marriage to enter the highest level of the celestial heaven. To LDS readers, this should all sound very familiar because it is part of Mormon doctrine.

Other notable teachings of Swedenborg include the claim that the original church died spiritually, thus creating the need for the Lord to establish a new church; the concept that man is not saved by faith alone but must show works from a changed heart; and that "God is very man." (https://lastchurch.com/dlw11_13.html). The similarities between these teachings and Joseph Smith's teachings are too strong to be a coincidence. (For more examples of Joseph Smith's "borrowed" doctrine, see https://youtu.be/AJTxk9W2fxQ)

The Form of God

Mormon doctrine states that God the Father has a physical body of "flesh and bone" (D&C 130:22), and that He once lived in human form on another planet, where He was resurrected. He progressed to become our God, our literal Father in heaven. The continuation of this doctrine is that we, too, can become future gods of other planets.

> *...He was once a man like us; yea, that God himself, the Father of us all, dwelt on an earth, the same as Jesus Christ Himself did... (History of the Church, volume 6, p. 305-306).*

> *God himself was once as we are now, and is an exalted man. ...I say, if you were to see him today, you would see him like a man in form – like yourselves, in all the person, image and very form as a man... (LDS founder Joseph Smith's History of the Church, volume 6, p. 305, and also Teachings of the Prophet J. Smith, p. 345).*

What does the Bible say regarding God and His form?

> *John 4:24 (KJV): God is a Spirit and they that worship him must worship him in spirit and in truth.*

Interestingly enough, the Book of Mormon agrees with the Bible in this matter:

> *Alma 18:26-29: And then Ammon said: Believest thou that there is a Great Spirit? And he said, Yea. And Ammon said: This is God.*

Alma 31:15: Holy, holy God; we believe that thou art God, and we believe that thou art holy, and that thou wast a spirit, and that thou art a spirit, and that thou wilt be a spirit forever.

Early in the history of the LDS Church, Joseph Smith taught that God is a spirit, as stated in the Book of Mormon and the early Doctrine and Covenants. The original 1835 edition of the Doctrine and Covenants had a section titled "Lectures on Faith." This section was removed in 1921. You might ask why it was removed. In part, perhaps, due to the following statement (Lectures on Faith, lecture 5):

*There are two personages who constitute the great, matchless, governing, and supreme power over all things—by whom all things were created and made that are created and made, whether visible or invisible; whether in heaven, on earth, or in the earth, under the earth, or throughout the immensity of space. They are the Father and the Son: **The Father being a personage of spirit**, glory, and power, possessing all perfection and fullness. The Son, who was in the bosom of the Father, **a personage of tabernacle, made or fashioned like unto man, or being in the form and likeness of man**—or rather, man was formed after his likeness and in his image. He is also the express image and likeness of the personage of the Father, possessing all the fullness of the Father, or the same fullness with the Father, being begotten of him.*

If this were left in the Doctrine and Covenants, it would directly contradict Doctrine and Covenants 130:22 (quoted previously), which states that the Father has a body of flesh and bone. The teaching that God has a physical body came with the officially accepted version of Joseph Smith's first vision story, published in 1840 (see Chapter 10, "Joseph Smith and the First Vision").

The Father is known as "the Invisible God" throughout the Bible (for example, in Colossians 1:15). The Father has this title because Human eyes cannot see him.

> 1 John 4:12 (KJV): *No man hath seen God at any time. If we love one another, God dwelleth in us, and his love is perfected in us.*

> John 1:18 (NIV): *No one has ever seen God, but the one and only Son, who is himself God and is in closest relationship with the Father, has made him known.*

And the words of our savior …

> John 6:46: *No one has seen the Father except the one who is from God [the Savior referring to himself here]; only he has seen the Father.*

Joseph Smith claimed that God the Father and the Son visited him together. That is a lot to ask a person to accept, especially considering that from the time of Adam up through the time of the writings above in the New Testament, only Christ had seen the Father. Are we to believe Joseph Smith was the only person other than Christ to see the Father?

I came across an interesting statement by former LDS prophet Gordon B. Hinckley on the subject of God once being a man. His statement attempts to downplay what the church taught for over a century. In a 1997 interview with the San Francisco Chronicle, he was asked if God was once a man. He responded as follows:

> *I wouldn't say that. There was a little couplet coined, 'As man is, God once was. As God is, man may become.' Now that's more of a couplet than anything else. That gets into some pretty deep theology that we don't know very much about.*[9]

I am curious to know why there was such a shift in this doctrine. Could the doctrine be targeted for a possible reversal? It will be interesting to see where this goes in the years ahead. Given that Hinckley was the prophet at the time of the "We are Christians too" campaign (several speakers at the LDS 177th Annual General Conference echoed this message of "Mormons as Christians"), I cannot help but wonder if this statement was part of President Hinckley's attempt to have Mormonism accepted as a Christian faith.

Only One God

As previously stated, LDS doctrine teaches that we can progress to godhood. The Mormon prophet Lorenzo Snow once coined the couplet that Hinckley referred to: "As man is, God once was, as God is, man may be." Is this an eternal possibility for us humans? Are we "gods in embryo"?

Spencer W. Kimball, the twelfth president of the LDS church, stated:

> *Brethren, 225,000 of you are here tonight. I suppose 225,000 of you may become gods. There seems to be plenty of space out there in the universe. And the Lord has proved that he knows how to do it. I think he could*

make, or probably have us help make, worlds for all of us, for every one of us 225,000. [10]

Let's turn again to the Bible, our blueprint for truth. The prophet Isaiah is crystal clear on this:

Isaiah 43:10 (KJV): ... *before me there was no God formed, neither shall there be after me.*

Isaiah 44:6,8 (KJV): *Thus saith the LORD the King of Israel, and his redeemer the LORD of hosts; I am the first, and I am the last; and beside me there is no God. Fear ye not, neither be afraid; have not I told thee from that time, and have declared it? ye are even my witnesses.* **Is there a God beside me? Yea, there is no God; I know not any**.

Isaiah 46:9 (NIV): ...**I am God, and there is none else; I am God, and there is none like me**.

In his book *"The Purpose Driven Life,"* author Rick Warren stated the following:

Let me be absolutely clear: You will never become God, or even a god. That prideful lie is Satan's oldest temptation. Satan promised Adam and Eve that if they followed his advice, "ye shall be as gods." Many religions and New Age philosophies still promote this old lie that we are divine or can become gods.

Where did the LDS doctrine of multiple gods come from? Even the Book of Mormon teaches that there is only one God. Not a single verse refers to multiple gods. Here is one example:

> Alma 11:26-29: *And Zeezrom said unto him: Thou*
> *sayest there is a true and living God? And Amulek*
> *said: Yea, there is a true and living God. Now Zeezrom*
> *said: Is there more than one God? And he answered,*
> *No.*

We also see the following in the "Testimony of the Three Witnesses" (introduction to the Book of Mormon):

> *And honor be to the Father, and to the Son, and to the*
> *Holy Ghost, which is one God.*

The doctrine that we can become gods, or that the Father, the Son, and the Holy Ghost are separate gods, was not taught in the early days of Mormonism. The Book of Mormon was written before the church was established, which is likely why it aligns with the Bible in its belief in one God. As the church evolved, however, new and unique doctrines came along, including the doctrine that we can progress to godhood.

The common LDS title for the Father, the Son, and the Holy Ghost is "The Godhead." The term "Godhead" is found three times in the King James Version: Acts 17:29, Romans 1:20, and Colossians 2:9. I have also heard Dr. Charles Stanley use the term "Godhead" to describe the three "persons" of God. It might seem odd to refer to multiple "persons" as one, but consider this: the Bible speaks of the husband and wife as one, and the church as one.

I will be the first to admit that the Christian teaching on who God is can be challenging to comprehend. This concept was difficult for me to accept as I transitioned into mainstream Christianity, but I have come to understand that it is indeed biblical.

The most precise definition of God that I could find was in an Internet article titled "Our Triune God" by John MacArthur (www.gty.org). Here are some quotes from the article:

> *The Trinity is an unfathomable, and yet unmistakable doctrine in Scripture. As Jonathan Edwards noted, after studying the topic extensively, 'I think [the doctrine of the Trinity] to be the highest and deepest of all Divine mysteries'" (An Unpublished Treatise on the Trinity). Yet, though the fullness of the Trinity is far beyond human comprehension, it is unquestionably how God has revealed Himself in Scripture—**as one God eternally existing in three Persons.***

> *This is not to suggest, of course, that the Bible presents three different gods (cf. Deut. 6:4). Rather, **God is three Persons in one essence**; the Divine essence subsists wholly and indivisibly, simultaneously and eternally, in the three members of the one Godhead— the Father, Son, and Holy Spirit…*

> *In describing the Trinity, the New Testament clearly distinguishes three Persons who are all simultaneously active. They are not merely modes or manifestations of the same person (as Oneness theology incorrectly asserts) who sometimes acts as Father, sometimes as Son, and sometimes as Spirit. At Christ's baptism, all three Persons were simultaneously active (Matt. 3:16-17), with the Son being baptized, the Spirit descending, and the Father speaking from Heaven. Jesus Himself prayed to the Father (cf. Matt. 6:9),*

*taught that His will was distinct from His Father's
(Matt. 26:39), promised that He would ask the Father
to send the Spirit (John 14:16), and asked the Father
to glorify Him (John 17:5). These actions would not
make sense unless the Father and the Son were two
distinct Persons. Elsewhere in the New Testament,
the Holy Spirit intercedes before the Father on behalf
of believers (Rom. 8:26), as does the Son, who is our
Advocate (1 John 2:1). Again, the distinctness of each
Person is in view. [11]*

As a Mormon, it seemed to me that the church attempted to
define God in a literal and rational way using human understanding. For example, in LDS teaching, the Genesis verse that
states man was made in "God's image" means that we simply
look like God. Is the meaning of "image" really that literal in
this scripture? What does it mean to be created in God's image?

I believe being "created in God's image" is far deeper than
our physical appearance and demonstrates that God created us
with some of the same attributes He possesses. These attributes
include the ability to love, to feel compassion, and to serve.

Chapter 7

LATTER-DAY WORKS AND THE PRIESTHOOD

Temples and Temple Work

LDS members are encouraged to do temple work. This refers partly to performing saving ordinances for those who have lived on this earth and passed before us. The teaching is that those who died and did not receive Christ and His ordinances (for example, baptism) rely on the living to perform those ordinances on their behalf vicariously. The spirits of those who have passed away can then accept these ordinances as if they had accepted them while they were alive. Eternal marriages are also performed in LDS temples, both for the living and the dead.

As you might imagine, performing these ordinances for the billions of men and women who lived before us is daunting. Mormons spend countless hours in temples all over the world performing these ordinances. These are some of the "works" performed by those in the LDS faith. But are these ordinances essential?

Acts 17:24-25: *The God who made the world and everything in it is the Lord of heaven and earth and does not live in temples built by human hands. And he is not served by human hands, as if he needed anything...*

I believe God does not rely on man to bring His plans to fruition. He is not dependent on us, but instead, we are dependent on Him. He has been in control and always will be.

What were the temples of the Old Testament used for? Were the same ordinances performed in them as are performed in LDS temples? I found the following on IRR.org (Institute for Religious Research):

By His shed blood on the cross, Jesus satisfied the demands of God's law on behalf of guilty sinners, as pictured in the Old Testament animal sacrifices. Based on Christ's completed work, the Holy Spirit has been poured out on God's people in a new way, so that the Christian church—all those who truly cling to Christ alone in heartfelt faith—is the 'body of Christ,' a spiritual temple in which God now dwells.

None of the ordinances performed in Mormon temples, such as endowments, baptism for the dead, and eternal marriage, were performed in the Biblical temple; *its function was making atonement for sins as a precondition to worshiping the true and living God.* ***Jesus replaced the Old Covenant, of which the biblical temple was a part***. *He established a New Covenant based on His* *once-for-all atoning sacrifice, and under which He now serves as the 'great high priest' in the very sanctuary of heaven (Hebrews 4:14-16).* **A New Testament temple building is therefore a contradiction in terms, for it ignores the finished work of Christ, and harks back to the Old Covenant.**

The LDS Church also teaches that temple work will continue into the millennium and that there will be a temple (or temples) within the city of the New Jerusalem.

Doctrine and Covenants 84:2-4:

Yea, the word of the Lord concerning his church, established in the last days for the restoration of his people, as he has spoken by the mouth of his prophets, and for the gathering of his saints to stand upon Mount Zion, which shall be the city of New Jerusalem. Which city shall be built, beginning at the temple lot, which is appointed by the finger of the Lord, in the western boundaries of the State of Missouri, and dedicated by the hand of Joseph Smith, Jun., and others with whom the Lord was well pleased. Verily this is the word of the Lord, that the city New Jerusalem shall be built by the gathering of the saints, beginning at this place, even the place of the temple, which temple shall be reared in this generation.

I want to bring two aspects of this LDS scripture to your attention. First, it states that the city "shall be built." Second, it specifically mentions a "temple" that will be built within the city. What does the Bible tell us about the city of New Jerusalem?

Revelation 21 provides a detailed description of the city's size, composition, and origin.

> Revelation 21:1-2 (KJV): *And I saw a new heaven and a new earth: for the first heaven and the first earth were passed away; and there was no more sea. And I John saw the holy city, new Jerusalem, coming down from God out of heaven, prepared as a bride adorned for her husband.*

According to this passage of Scripture, the New Jerusalem shall come down "out of heaven." It will not be built by human hands.

> Revelation 21:22 (KJV): *And I saw no temple therein: for the Lord God Almighty and the Lamb are the temple of it.*

This verse clearly states that there will be no temple in the New Jerusalem and explains why it will be unnecessary.

So, how can the LDS and biblical descriptions of the New Jerusalem be so contrary? It gets very confusing, but when referring to the "New Jerusalem," Mormons immediately think of Missouri, where Joseph Smith declared a New Jerusalem would be built before the return of the Savior. This differs from the holy city, the New Jerusalem, referred to in the Book of Revelation.

Mormon doctrine declares that temple work will be performed throughout the Millennium after Christ's return from within the "New Jerusalem" in Missouri. Is it not interesting that the New Jerusalem promised in Revelation does not need a temple?

Baptism for the Dead

As mentioned at the beginning of this chapter, one of the ordinances practiced in LDS temples is "baptism for the dead." The LDS doctrine is that all people born on this earth must be physically baptized by immersion as a requirement for salvation (and this baptism must be performed by someone holding the proper priesthood authority).

In the temples, these baptisms are performed by proxy, meaning that living individuals can be baptized in the name of someone who has passed away. The belief is that each deceased individual who has not yet accepted Jesus Christ has the opportunity in "Spirit Prison" to accept the proxy baptism as their own (and in so doing, they accept Jesus Christ as their Savior) (see Chapter 8, "The LDS Plan of Salvation"). This baptism for the dead is one of the reasons that Mormons spend countless hours doing genealogy (tracing their family trees).

One scripture the LDS use to support this belief of required baptism for salvation is found in John 3:3-8, which states we must be born of water and spirit.

> Jesus replied, "Very truly I tell you, no one can see the kingdom of God unless they are born again." "How can someone be born when they are old?" Nicodemus asked. "Surely they cannot enter a second time into their mother's womb to be born!" Jesus answered, "Very truly I tell you, no one can enter the kingdom of God unless they are born of water and the Spirit. Flesh gives birth to flesh, but the Spirit gives birth to spirit. You should not be surprised at my saying, 'You must be born again.' The wind blows wherever it pleases. You hear its sound, but you cannot tell where it comes from or where it is going. So it is with everyone born of the Spirit."

Are these verses saying that baptism is required for salvation? Is that what being "born of water" means?

We previously learned that salvation comes through faith alone, a message repeated throughout the Bible. Therefore, being born of water cannot refer to baptism.

Multiple opinions exist regarding what it means to be "born of water." In verse 6, it appears that Jesus is contrasting two births— "flesh" (our completed physical birth) and "spirit" (our required spiritual birth). In verse 5, He says we must be born of "water" and "spirit." Comparing verses 5 and 6, we see that being "born of water" may refer to being "born of flesh," or our physical birth.

A second opinion suggests that "water" refers to the Holy Spirit, as seen in phrases like "rivers of living water" (John 7:38-39). This may not make sense initially because verse 5 would then refer to the spirit twice, making it redundant. The word "and" in verse 5, however, could have also been translated as "even," making the verse read "…unless they are born of water, even the Spirit" [12]

The spiritual birth was the focal point of Christ's message to Nicodemus here, as evidenced by the charge to be "born again" or "born from above." Jesus was trying to impart the critical message of being born spiritually.

What does it mean to be "born again"? Here is part of what Billy Graham had to say on the subject:

> *Being born from above is a supernatural act of God. The Holy Spirit convicts us of our sin; He disturbs us because we have sinned against God. And then the Holy Spirit regenerates us. That is when we are born again. The Holy Spirit comes to live in our hearts to*

help us in our daily lives. The Spirit of God gives us assurance, gives us joy, produces fruit in our lives and teaches us the Scriptures."

He went on to say:

To be born again means that '[God] will give you a new heart and put a new spirit within you' (Ezekiel 36:26). "Old things have passed away; behold, all things have become new" (2 Corinthians 5:17). We are "partakers of the divine nature" (2 Peter 1:4); we have "passed from death into life" (John 5:24). The new birth brings about a change in our philosophy and manner of living. [13]

It is not my intent to detract from the incredible experience of being baptized. Baptism is an opportunity to demonstrate our devotion to Jesus Christ outwardly, and we should be baptized through obedience. We are signaling to everyone around us and to God that we have accepted Jesus Christ as our Savior, repented of our sins, and committed ourselves to obeying God's commandments.

In my LDS training, I was taught to cite 1 Corinthians 15:29 as support for the practice of "baptism for the dead."

Else what shall they do which are baptized for the dead, if the dead rise not at all? Why are they then baptized for the dead?

This verse is the only biblical reference to baptism for the dead. There are varying opinions among experts regarding what baptism for the dead means. One of the most popular beliefs is that "baptized for the dead" was a metaphor for martyrdom.

The martyrdom metaphor is particularly apt when considering 1 Corinthians 15:29, especially in light of the verses that immediately follow, which refer to the suffering Paul himself endured.

When Paul wrote 1 Corinthians, the persecution of Christ followers was widespread. In many cases, believers would be martyred around the time they were baptized. Therefore, being "baptized for the dead" might have been a term describing the replacement of a fallen believer with a new believer's baptism.

The Priesthood

One of the LDS church's strongest claims to having the "fullness of the gospel" is its proclamation that it possesses God's holy priesthood. They proclaim boldly that they possess both the Aaronic Priesthood (from the biblical Levitical Priesthood) and the higher Melchizedek Priesthood (Abraham paid his tithes to Melchizedek).

Joseph Smith claimed both of these priesthoods were restored via two visitations. First, John the Baptist (as a resurrected being) visited Joseph Smith and Oliver Cowdery on May 15, 1829, and imparted the Aaronic Priesthood to them through the "laying on of hands." Second, Joseph Smith claims that Peter, James, and John later visited him and Oliver Cowdery, imparting the Melchizedek Priesthood.

The LDS believe this priesthood power gives them the right to act in God's name in performing ordinances, such as baptism, and proclaiming blessings, such as healing the sick. Claiming the sole possession of these priesthoods (and stating that no other modern church possesses them) also confirms the LDS in their belief that they are God's "only true church."

If the LDS claim is correct, and they are the only church on earth to have God's holy priesthood, then I would agree that they are God's only true church. But this claim needs to be reviewed carefully.

Let's look first at the Aaronic (or Levitical) priesthood. In the Book of Leviticus, the priesthood is established. Priests, primarily from the line of Aaron, were responsible for offering sacrifices, teaching the Law, and mediating between God and the people. You couldn't hold the priesthood unless you were a male born into the tribe of Levi. This has never changed. Only Levites could hold the Levitical priesthood throughout the Old and New Testaments.

A common view among mainstream Christianity is that the Levitical priesthood was never intended to be permanent (Hebrews 7:11). Because Christ fulfilled the Old Covenant, of which the Levitical priesthood was part, there was no longer a need for it. Jesus alone serves as the Great High Priest (Hebrews 4:14).

In the LDS faith, the Aaronic (Levitical) priesthood is conferred upon male individuals, regardless of their lineage. LDS revelation states that one must only be worthy of the priesthood.

It's hard for me to accept that the biblical priesthood of Aaron and the LDS Aaronic priesthood are the same. Today, twelve-year-old Mormon boys can receive the Aaronic Priesthood and be ordained to the office of Deacon. 1 Timothy 3:12 says, "deacons are to be husbands of one wife, ruling their children and their own houses well." Even LDS President Brigham Young claimed that Deacons were to be married:

It is not the business of an ignorant young man, of no experience in family matters, to inquire into the circumstances of families, and know the wants of every person ... it is not the business of boys to do this; but select a man who has got a family to be a

Deacon, whose wife can go with him, and assist him in adminis-
tering to the needy in the ward.... I will venture to say the view I
take of the matter is not to be disputed or disproved by Scripture
or reason (Journal of Discourses 2:89).

And what of the higher Melchizedek Priesthood? What do we know about it? Truthfully, not much. In the Bible, Melchizedek and Jesus Christ are the only individuals mentioned as holders of this priesthood. Hebrews 7 extensively discusses Jesus as a high priest "after the order of Melchizedek."

LDS revelation states that men can be ordained to the Melchizedek Priesthood. The claim is that all of the prophets in the Bible had this priesthood (The Words of Joseph Smith, p. 59). However, nothing in the Bible supports this. Mormonism teaches that Peter, James, and John held the Melchizedek Priesthood, but such claims are entirely without biblical support.

My father ordained me an Elder in the Melchizedek Priesthood when I was eighteen (I received the Aaronic Priesthood at age twelve). I want to say that my ordinations were spiritual experiences, like my baptism, but they were not. I never sensed any power or authority as a priesthood holder. Yet, since I was told I had this authority, I did not doubt.

As a Mormon, I was a little perplexed as to why we would need two separate methods for healing—prayer and priesthood blessings. I always believed that prayer and faith alone were the necessary ingredients for healing.

The Mormon Church's hierarchy is established through the LDS priesthood. The Prophet is the head of the church, followed by twelve apostles and other world leaders, and then by local congregational leaders, known as Bishops.

To me, it seems that the Mormon faith, in some respects, did not move forward to the changes Christ brought us under the new covenant. And just what would those changes be regarding the priesthood?

In the Old Covenant, priests would intercede on behalf of sinful people with God. In the new covenant, we have all been given direct access to God, our great High Priest alone.

> 1 Timothy 2:5 (KJV): *For there is one God, and one mediator between God and men, the man Christ Jesus.*

> Hebrews 7:23-28 (NIV): *Now there have been many of those priests, since death prevented them from continuing in office; but because Jesus lives forever, he has a permanent priesthood. Therefore he is able to save completely those who come to God through him, because he always lives to intercede for them.*

> *Such a high priest truly meets our need—one who is holy, blameless, pure, set apart from sinners, exalted above the heavens. Unlike the other high priests, he does not need to offer sacrifices day after day, first for his own sins, and then for the sins of the people. He sacrificed for their sins once for all when he offered himself.* **For the law appoints as high priests men in all their weakness; but the oath, which came after the law, appointed the Son**, *who has been made perfect forever.*

Chapter 8

THE LDS PLAN OF SALVATION

I wrote this chapter last. I considered doing something like this when a friend asked me, "Do you mention the different Mormon heavens in your book?" I then realized it would help the reader understand what Mormons believe regarding the "big plan." This can get complex, but I will attempt to explain it as plainly as possible.

The LDS view of salvation and the afterlife, which they term "The Plan of Salvation," has many levels. For example, it does not merely end in Heaven or Hell as our final dwelling place. The diagram below is a reasonably accurate representation of what I was taught in the LDS Church regarding God's "plan of salvation."[14]

Reviewing the diagram, you will likely recognize some familiar elements from your Bible studies, such as Paradise, the Millennium, and the Final Judgment. You are also likely to encounter some concepts you have never come across (if you are a non-LDS reader), such as our existence as "Intelligences," "Spirit Prison," and the three separate kingdoms of heaven.

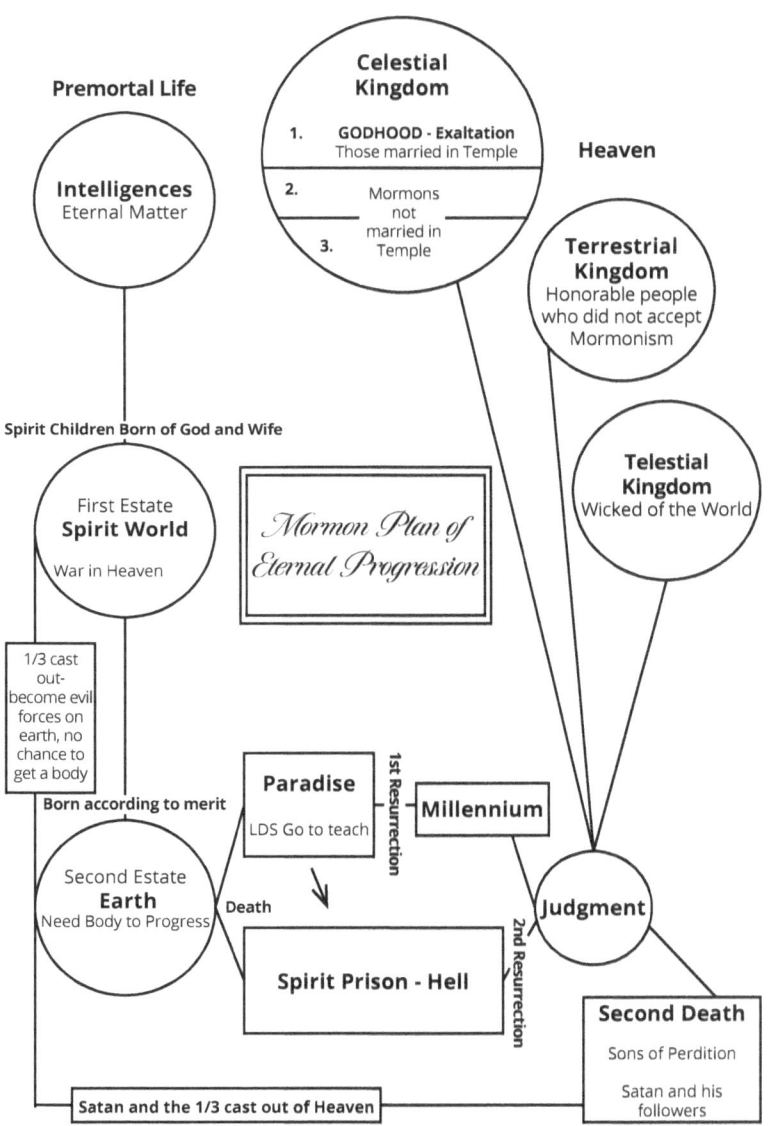

Premortal Life

Celestial Kingdom

1. GODHOOD - Exaltation
Those married in Temple

2. Mormons not married in Temple

3.

Heaven

Intelligences
Eternal Matter

Terrestrial Kingdom
Honorable people who did not accept Mormonism

Spirit Children Born of God and Wife

Telestial Kingdom
Wicked of the World

First Estate
Spirit World

War in Heaven

Mormon Plan of Eternal Progression

1/3 cast out- become evil forces on earth, no chance to get a body

Born according to merit

Paradise

LDS Go to teach

1st Resurrection

Millennium

Second Estate
Earth
Need Body to Progress

Death

Spirit Prison - Hell

2nd Resurrection

Judgment

Second Death

Sons of Perdition

Satan and his followers

Satan and the 1/3 cast out of Heaven

The LDS believe our existence did not start on this earth (depicted on the left side of the diagram). LDS doctrine teaches that we were eternal "intelligences" (with no beginning). Later, we were born spiritually to our heavenly Father and a heavenly Mother (our "First Estate" in a premortal world, often referred to as the "Pre-Existence"). The doctrine goes on to state that Satan rebelled against God in this premortal world, and one-third of our spirit brothers and sisters were cast out with him (down to earth).

Next, according to LDS scripture, we were born on this earth (our "Second Estate") to be "tried and tested" (although some of us have an advantage on earth based on our level of obedience in the pre-existence).

> D&C 138:55-56: *I observed that they were also among the noble and great ones who were chosen in the beginning to be rulers in the Church of God. Even before they were born, they, with many others, received their first lessons in the world of spirits and were prepared to come forth in the due time of the Lord to labor in his vineyard for the salvation of the souls of men.*

According to the LDS Plan of Salvation, what happens after death is also complex. Based on how we "perform" on earth, we go to one of two places (no, not heaven or hell). Those who accepted Jesus Christ and lived righteously go to "Paradise," and everyone else goes to "Spirit Prison." These temporary dwelling places will exist only until the "Final Judgment," after which we move on to one of four final dwelling places.

The LDS teach that it is while in Spirit Prison that those who did not accept Christ while here on earth are taught the gospel and given one last chance to accept Christ as their savior. The "baptisms for the dead" performed in LDS temples (as discussed in the previous chapter) are presented to these individuals who have the option to accept or reject their baptism.

Three of the four places we might end up in are included under the umbrella of "heaven." These three "degrees of glory" are much nicer than Earth. The Celestial Kingdom, where God dwells, is the highest and our primary goal, followed by the Terrestrial Kingdom and finally the Telestial Kingdom.

The Celestial Kingdom itself is divided into three additional levels. Only those married in the temple will reach the highest level (Exaltation). Single people can only be angels; the topic of eternal marriage was covered in chapter 6.

Those who are genuinely evil, such as those who deny the Holy Ghost, have no part in heaven and are cast out into "Outer Darkness," where they suffer and are under the influence of Satan eternally. This is the "second death" or spiritual death (the unsaved who are separated from God).

As a Mormon, the LDS view of the Plan of Salvation made great sense to me. It was a doctrine with which I had no issues. It was deeper than other Christian views and seemed somehow fairer to me insofar as "good people" were not cast into hell and had a second chance to accept Jesus as their Savior. I always believed that a loving heavenly Father would do all He could to keep us from suffering eternally.

I am sure that when it comes to the next life, not even the Bible has all the answers. There are simply some questions that we will not have the answers to until after mortality. In His wisdom, God has shared with us what we need to know to guide us to where we need to be. Our focus should be on following Christ and helping others do the same.

As with every other topic we have visited, we should ask ourselves how the LDS plan of salvation compares with what the Bible teaches.

The LDS "Pre-existence" or "Premortal Life" Doctrine

Did we live as spirits before our physical birth on earth? Does the Bible teach this?

> Zechariah 12:1 (KJV): *The burden of the word of the Lord for Israel, saith the Lord, which stretcheth forth the heavens, and layeth the foundation of the earth, and formeth the spirit of man within him.*

> 1 Corinthians 15:46-47 (NIV): *The spiritual did not come first, but the natural, and after that the spiritual.*

According to the Bible, our spirits were created "within" our physical bodies. Mormons do not believe this and often use Jeremiah 1:5 (KJV) to demonstrate that we lived as spirits before we existed in earthly bodies. This verse states:

> **Before I formed thee in the belly I knew thee;** *and before thou camest forth out of the womb I sanctified thee, and I ordained thee a prophet unto the nations.*

Because God is omnipresent, He is present in every moment, past, present, and future. God is also omniscient (all-knowing) and, therefore, knows all of us before we are conceived. Because He is our Creator and Inventor, He created each of us with an individual purpose.

There is no biblical reference to a pre-existence or premortal life. This is a man-made idea. For more information, see www.gotquestions.org/pre-existence-of-souls.html

The LDS Doctrine of the Origin of Jesus Christ

Mormonism and mainstream Christianity are also at odds when it comes to doctrine regarding the origin of Jesus Christ. Where did He come from?

The LDS teaching is that Jesus Christ is our spiritual older brother, that He was born as God the Father's first spirit child in the pre-existence, and that we are also spirit children of our heavenly Father (and possibly our heavenly Mother or mothers). Hence, Christ is our older brother. Additionally, Lucifer is also our spiritual brother.

The teaching states that during this spiritual existence, God the Father wanted His children to progress further by entering an earthly existence where they could gain a physical body, develop faith, and prove themselves.

This phase of life on Earth was part of a pattern. As mentioned earlier, Mormons believe that God the Father once lived on an earth, where He developed and progressed.

The LDS teaching further states that, during our preexistence, two plans regarding our earthly existence were brought to the Father. One plan came from Jehovah. The plan he presented allowed all men to have free moral agency—that is, the capacity to choose good over evil. He offered Himself as a sacrifice, knowing that we would sin. He offered Himself but stated that all the glory would go to the Father.

The second plan presented to the Father came from Lucifer. The plan he presented would force all men to be obedient so that none would be lost. Lucifer's plan offered no free moral agency. Lucifer offered this plan and requested that the Father give him His glory through it.

LDS doctrine further states that the Father rejected Lucifer and his plan, casting him out of His presence. As a highly influential character, Lucifer took with him one-third of the hosts of heaven, his followers.

In other words, one-third of our spirit brothers and sisters followed Satan and left their heavenly home. The entire story is in the LDS "Book of Moses," which is in the Pearl of Great Price (Moses 4:1-4).

Let's examine the claim that our Savior is our spirit brother. Is this possible? What does the Bible say regarding the origin of Jesus Christ?

> John 1:1-3 (KJV): *In the beginning was the Word, and the Word was with God, and the Word was God. The same was in the beginning with God. All things were made by him; and without him was not any thing made that was made.*

In these verses, "the Word" refers to Jesus Christ. If "the Word" was God from "the beginning" (before anything was created), then how could He have been born or created as a spirit child of our heavenly Father? That would mean He did not always exist and was not God from the beginning.

Jesus Christ is the Creator, not the created.

> Revelation 1:7-8 (RSV): *Behold, he is coming with the clouds, and every eye will see him, every one who pierced him; and all tribes of the earth will wail on account of him. Even so. Amen. "I am the Alpha and*

the Omega," says the Lord God, "who is and who was and who is to come, the Almighty."

Further, Colossians 1:16-17 (RSV) states:

For in him all things were created, in heaven and on earth, visible and invisible, whether thrones or dominions or principalities or authorities—all things were created through him and for him. He is before all things, and in him all things hold together.

The LDS Doctrine of Paradise

In chapter 23 of the Gospel of Luke, we find the story of two thieves who were crucified alongside Jesus. In verses 42-43 (KJV), we read the words of one of those thieves:

*And he said unto Jesus, Lord, remember me when thou comest into thy kingdom. And Jesus said unto him, Verily I say unto thee, **Today shalt thou be with me in paradise**.*

This story is a beautiful example of God's grace. Here we see a man acknowledging that he is deserving of his crucifixion. In his last words, he confesses Jesus as Lord, and his authentic words of faith are a saving act. Indeed, he was not saved by his works, but by God's grace. The LDS church attempts to reinterpret the meaning of these verses, as they point to a doctrine that is not in alignment with their doctrine, which states that we are saved by grace, but only "after all we can do" (see Chapter 3, "More on Grace").

Joseph Smith said the following regarding the word "paradise" as used in verse 43:

*There has been much said by modern divines about the words of Jesus (when on the cross) to the thief, saying, "This day shalt thou be with me in paradise." King James' translators make it out to say paradise. But what is paradise? It is a modern word: it does not answer at all to the original word that Jesus made use of. Find the original of the word paradise. You may as easily find a needle in a haymow. Here is a chance for battle, ye learned men. There is nothing in the original word in Greek from which this was taken that signifies paradise; but it was—This day thou shalt be with me in the **world of spirits**. (Scriptural Teachings of the Prophet Joseph Smith, sel. Joseph Fielding Smith, page 309)*

Contrast this with the words of Greek Scholar A.T. Robertson regarding the subject of Paradise as used in Luke 23:43:

Today shalt thou be with me in Paradise (Σημερον μετ' εμου εση εν τω παραδεισω).

*However crude may have been the robber's Messianic ideas Jesus clears the path for him. He promises him immediate and conscious fellowship after death with Christ in Paradise which is a Persian word and is used here not for any supposed intermediate state; but **the very bliss of heaven itself**. This Persian word was used for an enclosed park or pleasure ground (so Xenophon). The word occurs in two other passages in the N.T. (2 Corinthians 12:4; Revelation 2:7), in both of which the reference is plainly to heaven.*

The LDS Doctrine of Three Degrees of Glory (Levels of Heaven)

According to LDS belief, the Apostle Paul briefly described the three degrees of glory.

> 1 Corinthians 15:40-42 (NLT): *There are also bodies in the heavens and bodies on the earth. The glory of the heavenly bodies is different from the glory of the earthly bodies. The sun has one kind of glory, while the moon and stars each have another kind. And even the stars differ from each other in their glory. It is the same way with the resurrection of the dead. Our earthly bodies are planted in the ground when we die, but they will be raised to live forever.*

I have read these verses numerous times to grasp their meaning. It appears to refer to the resurrection, highlighting that our earthly bodies are temporary and perishable, whereas our resurrected bodies are eternal and imperishable. Both of these "bodies" are described as having glory, as are other God-created "bodies" (the sun, the moon, and the stars), but with different levels of glory. What I do not see in these verses is a clear connection to heavenly dwelling "places" for our resurrected bodies, as Mormon doctrine states.

I spent a lunch break at the local Christian bookstore to seek clarity on this topic. I identified and compared the five fattest Bible commentaries, focusing on 1 Corinthians 15:40-41. Interestingly, four of the five skipped over verses 40 and 41. I guess the writers were also unclear and opted not to comment.

I did, however, find 1 Corinthians 15:40-41 covered in The Believer's Bible Commentary by William MacDonald. [15] I liked his answer on the topic (so I purchased his commentary):

15:41 *Most commentators agree that Paul is still emphasizing that the glory of the resurrection body will be different from the glory of the body which we have on earth at the present time. They do not think that verse 41, for instance, indicates that in heaven there will be differences of glory among believers themselves. However, we tend to agree with Holsten that "the way in which Paul emphasizes the diversities of the heavenly bodies implies the supposition of an analogous difference of glory between the risen. It is clear from other passages of Scripture that we shall not all be identical in heaven... there will be differences of reward granted at the judgment Seat of Christ according to one's faithfulness in service. While all will be supremely happy in heaven, some will have greater capacity for enjoying heaven. Just as there will be differences of suffering in hell, according to the sins that a man has committed, so there will be differences of enjoyment in heaven, according to what we have done as believers.*

To further demonstrate this concept of "differences of reward", I cite the following:

Revelation 22:12: *Look, I am coming soon! My reward is with me, and I will give to each person according to what they have done.*

I attended an excellent international men's Bible study program, Bible Study Fellowship (BSF), for approximately five years. I like the way they present this truth:

Grace does not mean that our works do not matter, but that believers, saved by grace and dependent on it, are able to live for God's glory and be rewarded when their works are taken into account. [16]

The topic of the LDS plan of salvation is vast. Volumes of books have been written on this subject. I have highlighted some fundamental yet significant issues with the LDS perspective.

I want to come back to a scripture that I refer to many times in this book:

Ephesians 2:8 (NIV): *For it is **by grace you have been saved**, through faith—and this is not from yourselves, **it is the gift of God.***

God brought us the good news of "the **Gift** of salvation," not a plan of works referred to as "the **Plan** of Salvation."

Chapter 9

RACISM IN THE LDS CHURCH

I mentioned earlier that I always had trouble with certain LDS doctrines. The truth is that some doctrines (and former doctrines) are embarrassing to most Mormons. I know I was embarrassed whenever anybody asked me about them.

A case in point is a doctrine changed in 1978 by then-LDS Prophet Spencer W. Kimball. Until that point, the church's practice was that black men could not be ordained to the priesthood. The LDS priesthood is believed to have been handed down from Jesus Christ to His apostles, who later passed it on to Joseph Smith (see Chapter 7, "Latter-day Works and the Priesthood").

So why was the priesthood withheld from black male members of the church? I heard two basic views on this topic as a Mormon. One view was that blacks are descendants of Cain, who was cursed, and, as such, the priesthood was withheld from his descendants as part of that curse. The second view held that blacks had not been as valiant for God in their pre-earth life. Both explanations are incredibly insulting and demeaning and not of God. Here are some statements to this point:

According to the doctrine of the church, the Negro, because of some condition of unfaithfulness in the spirit—or pre-existence, was not valiant and hence was not denied the mortal probation, but was denied the blessings of the priesthood. (Joseph Fielding Smith, April 10, 1963 "The Negro in Mormon Theology" page 3)

Those who were less valiant in the pre-existence and who thereby had certain spiritual restrictions imposed upon them during mortality are known to us as the Negroes. Such spirits are sent to earth through the lineage of Cain, the mark put upon him for his rebellion against God and his murder of Abel being a black skin. (Bruce McConkie, Mormon Doctrine, pp. 476-477)

It is interesting to note that the practice of withholding the priesthood from black men did not start with Joseph Smith but was introduced by the second Prophet of the church, Brigham Young. Brigham Young spoke on the topic in Salt Lake City on October 9th, 1859 (recorded in the Journal of Discourses 7:290-291):

The first man that committed the odious crime of killing one of his brethren will be cursed the longest of anyone of the children of Adam. Cain slew his brother. Cain might have been killed, and that would have put a termination to that line of human beings. This was not to be, and the Lord put a mark upon him, which is the flat nose and black skin

...and they never can hold the Priesthood or share in it until all the other descendants of Adam have received the promises and enjoyed the blessings of the Priesthood and the keys thereof

In seeking an official statement from the LDS Church, the best I could find was the following from www.churchofjesuschrist.org.[17]

The Church was established in 1830, during an era of great racial division in the United States. At the time, many people of African descent lived in slavery, and racial distinctions and prejudice were not just common but customary among white Americans. Those realities, though unfamiliar and disturbing today, influenced all aspects of people's lives, including their religion. Many Christian churches of that era, for instance, were segregated along racial lines. From the beginnings of the Church, people of every race and ethnicity could be baptized and received as members. Toward the end of his life, Church founder Joseph Smith openly opposed slavery. There has never been a Church wide policy of segregated congregations.

During the first two decades of the Church's existence, a few black men were ordained to the priesthood. One of these men, Elijah Abel, also participated in temple ceremonies in Kirtland, Ohio, and was later baptized as proxy for deceased relatives in Nauvoo, Illinois. There is no evidence that any black men were denied the priesthood during Joseph Smith's lifetime.

In 1852, President Brigham Young publicly announced that men of black African descent could no longer be ordained to the priesthood, though thereafter blacks continued to join the Church through baptism and receiving the gift of the Holy Ghost. Following the death of Brigham Young, subsequent Church presidents restricted blacks from receiving the temple endowment or being married in the temple.

Over time, Church leaders and members advanced many theories to explain the priesthood and temple restrictions. None of these explanations is accepted today as the official doctrine of the Church.

The question you should ask yourself is this: Would God's one true church exclude any race of people from all of God's blessings? The Israelites were indeed God's original "chosen" people. Still, from the time of the Apostle Paul, God commanded that the gospel —namely, the good news of salvation through Jesus Christ—be shared with the entire world, with "both Jew and Gentile" (i.e., if you are not a Jew, you are a Gentile). We are all children of God and loved equally by Him, regardless of race or any other distinction.

Galatians 3:28 (NIV): *There is neither Jew nor Gentile, neither slave nor free, nor is there male and female, for you are all one in Christ Jesus.*

Acts 10:34-35 (NIV): *Then Peter began to speak: I now realize how true it is that God does not show favoritism but accepts from every nation the one who fears him and does what is right.*

The Book of Mormon itself appears to support the teaching that dark skin color is a mark of a curse from God. For instance, the Book of Mormon states that the Lamanites were cursed with dark skin for their wickedness. Over several generations, the skin color of those Lamanites who became righteous gradually became whiter.

> Alma 3:6: *And the skins of the Lamanites were dark, according to the mark which was set upon their fathers, which was a curse upon them because of their transgression and their rebellion against their brethren…*

> 3 Nephi 2:15: *And their curse was taken from them, and their skin became white like unto the Nephites…*

To mitigate the apparent racism in the Book of Mormon, the LDS Church revised a verse in 1981.

> 2 Nephi 30:6: *And then shall they rejoice; for they shall know that it is a blessing unto them from the hand of God; and their scales of darkness shall begin to fall from their eyes; and many generations shall not pass away among them, save they shall be a pure and delightsome people.*

Before 1981, this verse concluded with "… they shall be a white and delightsome people."

In 1960, Spencer W. Kimball, then serving as an LDS apostle, spoke about the changing of skin color. His conference speech was titled "The Day of the Lamanites".[18]

The day of the Lamanites is nigh. For years they have been growing delightsome, and they are now becoming white and delightsome, as they were promised (2 Ne. 30:6). In this picture of the twenty Lamanite missionaries, fifteen of the twenty were as light as Anglos; five were darker but equally delightsome. The children in the home placement program in Utah are often lighter than their brothers and sisters in the hogans on the reservation.

At one meeting a father and mother and their sixteen-year-old daughter were present, the little member girl—sixteen— sitting between the dark father and mother, and it was evident she was several shades lighter than her parents—on the same reservation, in the same hogan, subject to the same sun and wind and weather.

There was the doctor in a Utah city who for two years had had an Indian boy in his home who stated that he was some shades lighter than the younger brother just coming into the program from the reservation. These young members of the Church are changing to whiteness and to delightsomeness

It is beyond belief that anybody can believe our skin color has anything to do with our righteousness or our standing with God. Changing the wording in the Book of Mormon is an apparent attempt to avoid this embarrassing association.

However, I credit the LDS leadership for turning from their earlier practices. They have taken steps in the right direction.

Gordon B. Hinckley, church president from 1995–2008, stated:

> *I remind you that no man who makes disparaging remarks concerning those of another race can consider himself a true disciple of Christ. Nor can he consider himself to be in harmony with the teachings of the Church of Christ. Let us all recognize that each of us is a son or daughter of our Father in Heaven, who loves all of His children.*

This is where I get a little personal. I felt a genuine connection with the African American people in the South. I began my missionary work just a few months after the LDS church reversed its policy regarding blacks and the priesthood. For this reason, I devoted considerable time to missionary work in predominantly African American neighborhoods.

I have never met humbler and more authentic people. Many had great faith and fantastic trust in God. It was wonderful to be among them.

Several years ago (long after my LDS mission), I received a phone call from one of my sisters who said she had some big news. Her genealogical research revealed that our second great-grandmother was at least partially of African descent.

Two sisters, a brother, and I were later DNA tested. According to my DNA results, I am approximately 4% black, primarily from the region around the Congo. I realize this goes way back in the family tree, but hearing the news was awesome.

If more people took the time to research their ancestry, they might be shocked at what they learn. DNA testing could prove to be a powerful tool in combating racism. When it comes to our ancestry, we are likely not exactly what we think we are. What is essential to understand is that we are all children of God, regardless of race or color. We are all alike in that we are created in the very image of God.

Chapter 10

JOSEPH SMITH AND THE FIRST VISION

J oseph Smith was the founder and first prophet of the
Church of Jesus Christ of Latter-day Saints (LDS Church).
To become a member, one must accept Joseph Smith as a
"Prophet, Seer, and Revelator," chosen by God, and accept all
the new scriptures and doctrines he introduced.

Joseph Smith claimed to have had a magnificent vision in
1820 while praying as a young teenager. This is known to church
members as "The First Vision." What Joseph witnessed in that
vision is unclear, as a few differing versions of the event exist.

I researched only LDS sources to obtain information regarding
the events of Joseph Smith's first vision. The following comes
from three different versions of the first vision story.

1832 Version, JS History, pp. 1-3:

> *I saw the Lord and he spake unto me saying Joseph*
> *my son thy sins are forgiven thee.*

In this version of the first vision, Joseph Smith mentions that he "saw the Lord," but he does not mention seeing God the Father or any angels.

1835 Version, JS Journal, pp. 9-11 November 1835, pp. 2324 (in Joseph Smith's writing):

> *...a personage appeard in the midst, of this pillar of flame which was spread all around, and yet nothing consumed, another personage soon appeard like unto the first, he said unto me thy sins are forgiven thee, he testifyed unto me that Jesus Christ is the son of God; and I saw many angels in this vision.*

This version refers to seeing many angels but does not mention seeing the Lord or God the Father.

1838-1856, JS *History*, volume A-1, pp. 2-3:

> *When the light rested upon me I saw two personages (whose brightness and glory defy all description) standing above me in the air. One of <them>spake unto me calling me by name and said (pointing to the other) "This is my beloved Son, Hear him."*

Did Joseph Smith see only the Lord Jesus Christ, angels only, or both Jesus Christ and God the Father, but no angels? Each account is different.

If I had a vision from God, I would like to think I would tell the story relatively the same every time, exactly as I remembered it. It would be hard to forget the basic details of something so wonderful and spectacular.

The church's official version of the first vision account is the last version, which includes the visitation of both the Father and the Son. However, the version directly from Joseph Smith's journal states that he saw only angels.

Brigham Young, the second president of the LDS Church, stated that the Lord did not visit Joseph Smith. About this vision, he said:

> *The Lord did not come with the armies of heaven...*
> *But He did send His angel to this same obscure person,*
> *Joseph Smith jun...and informed him that he should*
> *not join any of the religious sects of the day, for they*
> *were all wrong. (Journal of Discourses, 2:171)*

More evidence suggests that Joseph Smith did not see God the Father in his vision. An added footnote to Lecture 5 of Lectures on Faith states that Joseph Smith received "further light" on April 2, 1843 (see D&C 130:22). This further light was the revelation that the Father has a body of flesh and bone. How could it have been "further light" if Joseph Smith knew the Father had a body of flesh and bone via his first vision experience twenty-three years earlier?

There are many more inconsistencies among the versions of the first vision. For example, in the early versions, the object of Joseph's prayer was to receive forgiveness for his sins. In the later versions, he stated that he went to prayer to ask God which church he should join.

The following is from the church-published Ensign Magazine from January of 1985,[19]

> *On at least four different occasions, Joseph Smith*
> *either wrote or dictated to scribes accounts of his*

sacred experience of 1820. Possibly he penned or dictated other histories of the First Vision; if so, they have not been located. The four surviving recitals of this theophany were prepared or rendered through different scribes, at different times, from a different perspective, for different purposes and to different audiences. It is not surprising, therefore, that each of them emphasizes different aspects of his experience... Indeed, there are long-standing precedents for differing accounts of the same spiritual experience. For example, the four Gospels do not correspond exactly concerning the great events at the garden's empty tomb. There are variations as to the number of women and angels who were present and whether the angels were sitting or standing.

To contend that Joseph Smith gave different versions of his vision because he was speaking to "different audiences" with "different perspectives" for "different purposes" is, in my opinion, a weak argument. The versions vary too widely to make that argument credible. I do not believe that anyone with such an intense experience, which they believed came from God, would change the story, regardless of whom they were talking to. You would either speak the truth or not speak at all (such as not "casting your pearls before swine").

Also, consider who Joseph Smith's audience was when he wrote his account in his journal. Most people write very personal and honest information in their journals. If this were the case with Joseph Smith, his journal version would be closest to the truth. This version is consistent with Brigham Young's statement that Joseph Smith saw angels, but not God. There is also no claim in this version that all the existing churches were false.

To compare "differing accounts" of the same story from the Bible to Joseph Smith's "differing accounts" of the first vision is also a weak argument. Separate individuals wrote the biblical accounts, and the apparent contradictions may not be contradictions at all.

Consider the following from Biblegateway.com:

> *...many of the alleged contradictions in the Gospel accounts are rather easily reconciled. For example... In terms of whether there were/was one angel (Matthew) or two (John) at Jesus' tomb, have you ever noticed that whenever you have two of anything, you also have one? It never fails. Matthew didn't say there was only one. John was providing more detail by saying there were two.*

Again, different individuals wrote the Gospels, so it is understandable that some minor details differ due to differing perspectives. On the other hand, Joseph Smith was the sole source of the story of the first vision. His versions differ significantly in detail.

The first version of the first vision story was written in 1832, twelve years after Joseph Smith's experience. Nothing was published on the subject until 1840. It is quite possible that the story evolved into an increasingly spectacular tale during the twenty-year interval between the event and the first publication of the account.

The last version of the first vision story became the church's official version. This version required a new church to be organized because the doctrines regarding the godhead it introduced could be found nowhere else in Christianity. Additionally, in that version, Joseph Smith stated that he was told none of the existing churches were true, hence the need to reestablish God's "true" church on earth (see the section titled "The Great Apostasy" in chapter 6).

A few years ago, a church speaker stated, "Truth, by definition, must be exclusive." That stuck with me. It made a lot of sense. There can be only one truth. Either one of the versions of Joseph Smith's story is true or none are true, but they certainly cannot all be true.

We should also consider whether Joseph Smith's first vision experience was unique to him. Could any of his stories have been "borrowed" from other sources? I was shocked when I discovered that other individuals who lived around the same area and time as Joseph Smith recorded similar experiences. I came across the following examples from Richard Bushman's book *Joseph Smith: Rough Stone Rolling* (March 2007 edition, page 41):

> *In 1826 a preacher at the Palmyra Academy said he saw Christ descend "in a glare of brightness, exceeding ten fold the brilliancy of the meridian Sun."*

Compare this wording with Joseph Smith's wording from one of his visions (Joseph Smith, Wentworth letter):

> *Joseph stated he was "surrounded with a brilliant light which eclipsed the sun at noon-day".*

Could this wording be a coincidence? The descriptions are very similar.

Here's a second example of an individual claiming to have had a vision of God from *Joseph Smith: Rough Stone Rolling:*

Norris Stearns published an account in 1815 of two beings who appeared to him: "One was God, my Maker, almost in bodily shape like a man. His face was, as it were a flame of Fire, and his body, as it had been a Pillar and a Cloud…. Below him stood Jesus Christ my Redeemer, in perfect shape like man".

Note that this vision was published in 1815, five years before Joseph Smith's 1820 vision. Here, we see someone claiming to have had a visitation from both the Father and the Son together (similar to Joseph Smith's last version of the first vision). In both the Norris Stearns and Joseph Smith visions, the Father and Son appear in the form of men.

Chapter 11

SPIRITUAL WITNESSES

Generally, the first Sunday of each month is reserved for a special LDS meeting called "Fast and Testimony Meeting." During this meeting, members are encouraged to stand and bear testimony, sharing what they believe to be God's truth, as witnessed through the Holy Ghost. Certain key elements of an LDS testimony are encouraged as validation of the LDS Church. Most members who bear testimony include these key elements, which include a witness that:

- The Book of Mormon is true.

- God called Joseph Smith to restore the true Church.

- God called the current LDS Prophet, and we should heed his words.

- The LDS Church is the only "true and living church" today.

- Jesus Christ lives and is our Savior; through Him, we can be forgiven of our sins.

In almost all cases, the testimony bearer will use "I know that" to introduce the element they are testifying about. For example, they will say, "I know that the Book of Mormon is true."

The words "I know" are powerful, especially when compared to phrases like "I believe" or "I feel." To say that you know something is true is to say that you have no doubt and are absolutely certain.

The words "I know that" flow almost automatically when an LDS member is bearing testimony. This is ingrained from early childhood, and I was no exception. Often, a parent accompanies the child and whispers what the child should say when bearing their testimony. This way, parents believe they are helping their children "gain a testimony." One LDS belief holds that our testimony develops as we share it with others.

In the LDS Church, I found these testimonies from young children endearing. Reflecting on it now, I realize this practice is not right. Nobody should be told what they "know" to be true, not even a child. Testimony is a very personal thing between an individual and God.

As a Mormon youth, I "believed" what I was taught because I had no reason to doubt. I trusted in the testimonies of my parents and others in the church. I figured that as time went on, the Holy Ghost would testify to me regarding these various doctrines, piece by piece, as I studied and prayed, and I would eventually come to know these things to be true. That day never came.

I became an expert at avoiding testimony-giving. I wished I could bear testimony, but I did not know these things were true, except that Jesus Christ was my Savior. It bothered me that people around me had spiritual witnesses that I never experienced. I should clarify that I did receive answers to specific questions in prayer, but not to the key elements of Mormonism, such as the Book of Mormon and Joseph Smith.

Joseph Smith taught that the Holy Ghost would testify of the truth through a "burning in your bosom" and that we can "feel" when something is right.

> Doctrine & Covenants 9:8: *But, behold, I say unto you, that you must study it out in your mind; then you must ask me if it be right, and if it is right I will cause that your bosom shall burn within you; therefore, you shall **feel** that it is right.*

These are the key experiences Mormons seek when they turn to God in prayer. They seek a testimony that all of these elements they have been taught are true through the "burning in their bosom" and the "feeling" that they are true.

I believe the word "feeling" can be dangerous. This word has multiple meanings. A feeling can be a sensation, such as when I felt the Holy Spirit enter my body. However, a feeling can also be triggered by an emotion. Being led by our emotions is not only dangerous but simply wrong. We do not have to look far to see the unfortunate and, in some cases, even disastrous consequences that can result when people act on their emotions. If we want to feel something badly enough, we will probably eventually feel it if we are in the correct emotional state.

The Bible tells us that we should not rely on our feelings:

> Proverbs 28:26 (KJV): *He that trusteth in his own heart is a fool: but whoso walketh wisely, he shall be delivered.*

> Jeremiah 17:9 (RSV): *The heart is deceitful above all things, and desperately corrupt; who can understand it?*

I cannot refute the statement regarding the burning in your bosom. When the Holy Spirit touches me, I experience a sense of warmth or peace in my core. It is not an emotion but a sensation, and it is always accompanied by clarity of mind (a more focused mind with a clearing of unimportant things). I'm sure others experience the Holy Spirit in different ways.

We should all examine ourselves and reflect on how God has personally touched us. Ask yourself: What things has God manifested to me? Do you really "know" that these things are true? How do you know?

Does your testimony align with the Word of God (the Bible)? God tells us to "search the scriptures" (John 5:39). If something we "know" to be true is not in line with the Bible, then it is not God's truth.

Chapter 12

LOOKING BACK

There is so much good that I took from my life in the LDS faith. I was taught proper morals, to love God with all my heart, and to love my fellow man. I was taught that Jesus Christ is my savior and that I can be forgiven for my sins through Him. I was taught that the only way to Heaven is through the Savior. I was taught that the Holy Ghost (the Holy Spirit) will guide our decisions as we seek Him. I was taught a great many other proper teachings as a Mormon.

The LDS church is exceptionally well-organized. The same doctrinal lessons are taught across the entire worldwide church virtually the same day (at least within a week or two). They have their own welfare system, which cares for members in need. After natural disasters, they provide vast amounts of food, water, and other essential supplies to people in need. They teach that members should prepare themselves for hard times.

Christianity can learn a great deal by observing the LDS Church. As I have come into mainstream Christianity, I have not seen that same unity that I had grown accustomed to in Mormonism. It would be great if Christian congregations worldwide could be more connected and move in pace with one another.

However, despite the many benefits of the LDS faith, there is also much that is wrong. The Mormon way of thinking is very black and white. They believe they are right and that everyone else is wrong, which can lead to a self-righteous attitude. You are either 100 percent in or 100 percent out. **As a member, you are expected to accept all doctrines of The Church of Jesus Christ of Latter-day Saints**. Any variance is often thought of as being "swayed by the devil" (some family members have accused me of being swayed by the devil).

Jesus addressed the issue of self-righteousness in the parable of the Pharisee and the Publican who were going to the temple to pray (Luke 18:9-14). The Pharisee (very rules-driven) prayed how grateful he was that he had everything right and was not like the lowly publican. On the other hand, the publican prayed simply, "God, have mercy on me a sinner."

The Pharisees' approach closely resembles the Mormon way of thinking. They believed themselves to be right while everyone else around them was wrong. They thought themselves to be "God's chosen" people.

I fell into this trap myself. I recall thanking God in my younger years for being born into "His church" and, therefore, not having to search for the truth. The truth had been given to me, probably due to some righteous act or actions in my former spirit life.

There is a "Mormonism" (a belief among members not usually taught from the pulpit) that goes something like this: Those who are members of the LDS church are among the honorable spirits in the pre-existence. They are shown God's favor here on earth based on their obedience before birth.

This sort of thinking is in sharp contrast to the Christian way of thinking, which places us all "equally" as sinners.

Romans 3:23 (NIV): *For all have sinned and fall short of the glory of God.*

Ecclesiastes 7:20 (RSV): *Surely there is not a righteous man on earth who does good and never sins.*

This is an excellent spot for a gentle reminder: Humility is a valuable attribute. We owe everything we have to God.

Ephesians 2:8-9 (KJV): *For it is by grace you have been saved, through faith –* ***and this is not from yourselves****, it is the gift of God – not by works,* ***so that no one can boast****.*

A close friend introduced me to "Rise and Be Healed," a book on addiction by Peter McCall and Maryanne Lacy. This friend noticed parallels between what I told her about Mormonism and what she had read in the book. It is uncanny how close the book comes to describing Mormon thinking without tying it to Mormonism. Here is a paragraph that goes to this point:

...Religious addicts maintain an 'either/or' way of thinking which excludes the middle ground of truth. They insist on their interpretation of the Bible, and any other possibilities are ruled out. They have their 'pet scriptures' which they use to resolve the most complex problems with ease. They see everything either black or white, and interpret any questioning about the conclusions as a personal attack. They see people as either for them or against them. They insist that everything be interpreted their way or else it deserves condemnation.

Does the above paragraph about religious addicts sound familiar? Isn't this the stance that many LDS members take? I know I did. The authors go on to say:

> *...They are driven by rituals... are compelled to perform certain practices out of fear of condemnation. They are perfectionists who demand perfection of themselves and others... Religious addicts become religious abusers. They inflict their extreme beliefs onto others in such a way that shame, fear and resentment result...* **religious addicts are so taken up with their grandiosity and their specialness with God that they are oblivious to the fact that they have a problem**.

And my favorite thought from *Rise and Be Healed*:

> *The one characteristic that may apply to religious addicts more than to others is the* **need for open-mindedness**. *Most religious addicts have a very narrow perception of God and the scriptures. There is a need to loosen up and to be open to the idea that the truth may be bigger than they thought.* **The overwhelming message of the scriptures must replace narrow interpretations which distort the message and end up giving us a too-small image of God.**

As humans with puny minds, we will never be able to comprehend God and His greatness fully. Have an open mind, not a narrow one.

Does Mormonism Play a Part in Negative Behavioral Issues of Its Members?

I touched on this previously in chapter 4. Based on my personal experience and national statistics, the short answer is a definite "yes."

Several people, including psychology professionals, have told me that my behavior often tends toward a "passive-aggressive" approach. What does this mean, and could this issue be related to my upbringing and lifelong learning?

I read a fascinating article in *Sunstone Magazine* from April 12, 2013. In it, Professor Michael J. Stevens of Weber State University (Utah) recounts some interesting findings discovered when comparing Weber State students, a high percentage of whom are LDS, to students from across the country. [20]

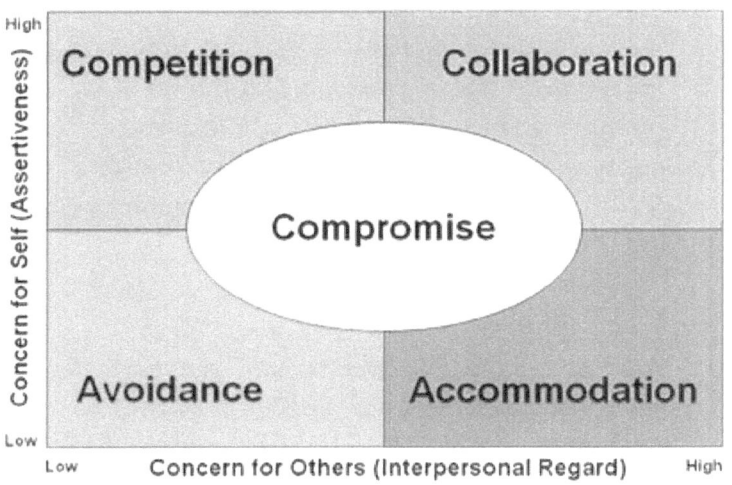

The article presents the findings of a study that sought to determine the students' preferred method of conflict resolution. The diagram above, from the article, illustrates the various methods of conflict resolution. Collaboration and Compromise are the most common methods nationally. The Avoidance method had a national average score of 4.0, but an average of 7.5 at Weber State University (with a possible range of 0 to 12). What is the significant difference between these Utah students and their peers nationally?

The author cited some possible reasons for this drastic difference. Here are a few:

> *Passive-aggression is the least common response option to conflict among the U.S. population at large and is typically viewed as an inadequate and unconstructive strategy (at least over the long term). It is generally used by those who would prefer that the conflict simply go away. One is passive in that one is unassertive in pursuing a resolution that addresses one's own interests and concerns, while simultaneously being aggressive—or better stated, while simultaneously being uninterested in, dismissive, or contemptuous of the needs or concerns of the other.*

> *A passive-aggressive person will generally deploy such behavioral tactics as: keeping one's distance and remaining silent or aloof; hiding one's true thoughts, feelings, or emotions; suppressing, setting aside, or ignoring issues that otherwise should be addressed; postponing or ignoring decisions; resisting change*

and otherwise championing the status quo; **citing rules, policies, procedures, or higher authority** *as both a defensive and offensive tactic; and providing little meaningful or worthwhile feedback.*

If all conflict is viewed as the functional equivalent of having the 'spirit of contention,' (from 3 Nephi 11:29 in the Book of Mormon) what options are left to a person who disagrees, or sees things differently, or who has goals and interests different from the rest of the community? **How can one raise objections or question and challenge others, or raise unpleasant topics, if doing so is tantamount to being in league with Beelzebub?** *If one's view of all conflict is that it must be avoided so as to avoid contention, then there is no direct, healthy, constructive strategy available for resolving conflicts and disagreements.*

A second possible source for the elevated rates of passive aggression among Latter-day Saints is its strong **culture of obedience and submission**. *A simple search of general conference talks for the past decade shows obedience to be a constant and recurring theme. For example, search queries at www.lds.org for variations of 'obey/obedience,' and 'submit/submission' returned over 500 hits in general conference talks since 2002, and Mosiah 3:19 (which encourages the reader*

to be 'submissive, meek, humble, patient, full of love,
willing to submit to all things') was quoted at least
once in 17 of the preceding 20 general conferences—
and more typically by members of the First Presidency
or Quorum of the Twelve Apostles.

In addition to passive-aggressiveness, another mental health issue is prevalent in Mormonism: depression. Several studies have found a link between Mormonism and depression. One was cited in a Los Angeles Times article of February 20, 2002, titled "Study Finds Utah Leads Nation in Antidepressant Use." This study points to the pressures of Mormonism, especially for women, to explain the surprising findings.[21] The following is an excerpt from the article:

Doctors here have for years talked about the
widespread use of antidepressants in the state. But
there was no hard evidence until a national study
that tracked drug prescriptions came to an unexpected
conclusion:

Antidepressant drugs are prescribed in Utah more
often than in any other state, at a rate nearly twice
the national average.

Suicide goes hand in hand with depression. Utah has one of the highest suicide rates in the nation (along with other heavily LDS states such as Idaho). The CDC statistics I reviewed online for 2024 showed Utah with the seventh highest teen suicide rate in the nation and Idaho with the sixth highest.

This is a sad reality, but it doesn't surprise me. The pursuit of perfection brings tremendous pressure. Speaking from my own experience, I can say that the pressure is extreme for teen boys as they near the age at which they are expected to serve as LDS missionaries.

The amount of stress placed on Mormons to "be ye therefore perfect" (Matt. 5:48) is enormous. As I have reached out to other former Mormons, I have learned that this pattern was also present in their lives.

Throughout my adulthood, I felt consistent pressure to conform to the rules of Mormonism. Failure to do so would render me "unworthy" to participate in certain activities, such as attending the temple.

I also constantly feared that I was not doing enough to ensure my personal "exaltation." Under legalism, the questions that come to mind are: "Am I doing enough?" and "What more can I do to prove myself to God?"

I would consider the mental health issues suffered by so many of the LDS as negative fruits of LDS doctrine, and **these negative fruits can be tied directly to the incorrect teaching of grace**. Understanding this simple truth about grace can alleviate great stress: our **salvation is already secure through our faith and trust in the Savior**. This eliminates all uncertainty from the equation. This is why Christians who affirm this gospel of grace are filled with deep gratitude and joy, rather than stress and uncertainty.

And How Is My Thinking Now?

Immediately after leaving Mormonism, I couldn't help but wonder which of all God's churches/denominations is His "officially recognized" church. I suppose that part of my legalistic thought process led me to believe that only one official organization was worthy of bearing the name of Christ.

I thought: How will I ever find the truth if I spent fifty years moving in the wrong direction? Which church is it?

I am happy to report that, through God's help, the truth on this topic came to me rather quickly. It seemed that I heard exactly what I needed to hear at church every week, and as I read and prayed, the truth became clearer to me.

I now believe that the "church" comprises all genuine followers of Christ. We are part of the Body of Christ, bringing our unique talents and spiritual gifts. I recognize some differences between denominations, but for the most part, these differences are not significant and do not detract from the Bible's overarching message.

I consider myself a relatively logical person. This is probably one of the reasons I became a computer programmer. My logical side tells me that if God decided to continue to have prophets on the earth to guide us, then what they tell us would complement the Bible, not contradict it. If the Bible is our blueprint, then anything that is not harmonious with it should be rejected. God is not a God of contradictions or confusion.

> 1 Corinthians 14:33 (KJV): *"For **God is not the author of confusion**, but of peace, as in all churches of the saints."*

Although I had felt for many years that something was not quite right in the Mormon faith, I wanted to be wrong. I wanted to develop a spiritual witness to the truthfulness of Mormon doctrine, to be fully committed and passionate about my faith, to share my convictions and testimony with my family and friends, and to experience happiness in my relationship with God; however, I never reached that point.

I believe that today it would take more and more faith to be a Mormon. I say this because of the things discussed earlier: the recent DNA evidence, the continuing lack of hard evidence supporting the Book of Mormon, Book of Mormon verses seemingly borrowed from the Bible, the issues with the Book of Abraham, the history of the LDS church regarding the different versions of the first vision story, and a myriad of other issues. Surely, God would provide us with evidence if it were true. God has given us vast amounts of evidence concerning the Bible's authenticity.

The Internet also portends some challenging times ahead for the Mormon Church. In the past, you would have had to visit a bookstore or library to research books that contradicted Mormon beliefs. The church has always taught its members to read only church-approved material regarding theology. On the Internet, however, you can research anything and have it at your fingertips in seconds. Most people are curious about church doctrine, as they should be. Everyone should be interested in getting to the truth.

I have always wanted to know God's truth. It took some time, but the Spirit led me to the truth, and things now line up for me. My logic and spiritual convictions finally align, bringing me great peace of mind.

Chapter 13

LOOKING FORWARD

How does living as a gospel of grace Christian differ from living as a Mormon? I can promise you that the cultures are very different, and it takes some getting used to. I am still getting my bearings. Here is a list of the most substantial differences I have experienced to date:

1–One word captures it: JOY. Joy because Gospel of Grace Christians realize that their salvation is complete. It was complete when they accepted Jesus Christ as their savior through faith, trusting in Him. This contrasts sharply with Salvation by Works believers, who worry that their efforts may not be sufficient to earn them a spot in heaven (or in the highest heaven). This stressful existence is not conducive to joy but rather to bondage. The truth sets you free, liberating you from all bondage.

2–Gospel of Grace Christians have wonderful attitudes. They do not have the hang-ups of legalism, wherein they feel the need to present themselves as better people than they are.

Christians are very open about their weaknesses because it is not about them (how good or bad they are) but about the sinless One who did what they could never do. Because Gospel of Grace Christians are more open, they are more likely to get support for their issues. Many Christian churches host a weekly program for people suffering from any addiction. This program is often referred to as "Celebrate Recovery." People will stand up in front of an entire group and share their struggles, seeking out others for support and accountability. This is all very healthy and based on scripture (see James 5:16). I found nothing close to this in the LDS culture. When Mormons have an addiction or a sin issue, they usually keep it very private and share it only with local church leadership.

3. Because Gospel of Grace Christians are more open and joy-filled, they are freer in their expression. Musical worship is often loud and spirited, which I have found actually to have biblical backing – Psalm 150:4-6:

   Praise Him with timbrel and dancing; Praise Him with stringed instruments and pipe. Praise Him with loud cymbals; Praise Him with resounding cymbals.

This form of praise is very different from the soft and reverent form of worship I grew accustomed to in Mormonism. It's been a long transition, but I have come to appreciate that neither form of musical worship is wrong; they are just different ways of praising God. I'm sure God appreciates all worship music because he loves variety, and each culture has its special way of worshiping. I sense that what matters is the hearts of the worshiping participants.

4–Because Christians are focused on the Bible as their only source of scripture, they have many wonderful teachings that I was never introduced to as a Mormon. Beyond the critical saving doctrines, the Bible is a valuable tool for living a happy, day-to-day life. It teaches us how to maintain proper relationships with others, cope with loneliness, deepen our relationship with God, cultivate patience, and many other invaluable lessons.

5–True Christianity leaves its members free to be themselves and, for the most part, does not try to mold people into a conformist group of homogeneous believers. To the contrary, we are all individual parts of the Body of Christ, and as such, we possess different gifts that benefit the whole. Individuality is welcomed and expected. Legalism, on the other hand, attempts to force everyone into the same mold. A new term I have become aware of since leaving Mormonism is "Mobots," which is a slang term that describes Mormons as robotic (insinuating being controlled and forced to conform so that they are all the same). While this is somewhat amusing, it is also sadly true. I have been accused of being "robot-like" myself, and I certainly see how my legalism has contributed to this perception. Being labeled as robotic is not a compliment. It suggests that I am not truly alive and not a free thinker, which makes me boring … yuck.

6–The universal symbol of Christianity is the cross. In the Mormon faith, the cross is not used. The late LDS Prophet Gordon B. Hinckley made the following statement in the April 2005 issue of the LDS Ensign magazine: "The cross is a symbol of the dying Christ, while our message is a declaration of the living Christ."[22] As a member, I bought into the common LDS belief that the cross was a "murder weapon" used to kill our savior and, therefore, should not be used as a symbol of belief. However, when I became a Gospel of Grace Christian, I began to rethink that. I believe there is no better reminder than the cross of the suffering Christ experienced for all of us. Galatians 6:14: "But God forbid that I should glory, **save in the cross of our Lord Jesus Christ**, by whom the world is crucified unto me, and I unto the world."

Final Words and Testimony

My current struggles include overcoming the effects that many years of passiveness and acceptance of a stressful, legalistic lifestyle have had on me. I hope that others will recognize they are trapped in a similar destructive cycle and fight their way out with determination. There is incredible freedom for those who are brave enough to fight. Know that you are not alone—that God will help you as He has helped other former LDS members who have found freedom.

Reflecting on all of this has made me realize that I would never have left Mormonism on my own. It took an unmistakable experience with the Holy Spirit to move me in the right direction, which may well be what it takes to move others. You, too, can have a witness from the Holy Spirit if you are honest in your prayers and seek the truth, but you must be open-minded and willing to accept God's truth when you receive it.

At the beginning of this journey, I thought my experiences leaving Mormonism were unique and my own. However, I have come to find that there are many others with very similar conversion stories. It comforts me that the Holy Spirit continues to turn the hearts of many to the truth. My prayer is that this conversion accelerates.

I am happy to report that I have not been alone. I owe a great deal to my daughter Cami, who left Mormonism several years before I did (she saw the issues early and fought Mormonism through high school). Cami, as your loving father, I can say with a smile that, although you were a real pain back in those days, I am incredibly proud of you now.

Many others have played important parts in my transformation. God put me on a path that connected me with the right people at the right time. God choreographed it all. None of it was a coincidence. Even today, I am making new Christian friends who help me in my walk with God. I am truly blessed and grateful to all of you.

Speaking from my own experience and background (and not in an arrogant sense), I believe that Mormons who convert to Gospel of Grace Christianity make fantastic Christians. Converting from Mormonism requires a focused seeker of truth, and seekers of truth will find freedom for their souls and a solid testimony of the Savior.

The Savior is real and alive and should be the number one focus of our lives. He is our creator and redeemer. We owe everything to Him. I intend to dedicate the rest of my life to serving Him.

I trust God completely and refuse to remain passive. I have chosen to replace "passive" with "passionate."

> Jeremiah 29:12-14 (RSV): *Then you will call upon me and come and pray to me, and I will hear you. You will seek me and find me; when you seek me with all your heart, I will be found by you, says the LORD...*

ENDNOTES

1. Rene Schlaepfer, Grace Immersion (2010)

2. https://www.patheos.com/resources/additional-resources/2010/08/mormons-and-the-bible-in-the-21st-century

3. Dr. Erwin W. Lutzer, Seven Reasons Why You Can Trust the Bible (Moody publishers, 1998)

4. The Institute for Creation Research (www.icr.org)

5. https://www.churchofjesuschrist.org/study/manual/book-of-mormon-teacher-resource-manual/the-introduction-to-the-book-of-mormon?lang=eng

6. https://www.beliefnet.com/faiths/christianity/latter-day-saints/2002/05/dna-research-and-mormon-scholars-changing-basic-beliefs.aspx

7. https://thoughtsonthingsandstuff.com/track-changes-the-sermon-on-the-mount-book-of-mormon-vs-new-testament/

8. John Gee, A History of the Joseph Smith Papyri and Book of Abraham (Brigham Young University, 1999) https://archive.bookofmormoncentral.org/content/history-joseph-smith-papyri-and-book-abraham

9. https://www.sfgate.com/news/article/SUNDAY-INTERVIEW-Musings-of-the-Main-Mormon-2846138.php

10. The Ensign Magazine, p. 80, November 1975

11. https://www.gty.org/library/Articles/A215/Our-Triune-God

12. William MacDonald, Believer's Bible Commentary (1992), 1478

13. https://billygraham.org/story/how-to-be-born-again

14. https://www.bing.com/images/earch?view=detail-V2&ccid=bNM8eM9i&id=24F66A2F0E2988C-2553D73EE5EE98B72BB759606&thid=OIP.bNM8eM9iDTniW60e7xSkUwHaFj&mediaurl=http%3a%2f%2f-www.utlm.org%2fimages%2feternalprogressionutlmthumb.gif&exph=150&expw=200&q=mormon+plan+of+salvation+chart&simid=608045370083706150&selectedIndex=75&ajaxhist=0

15. William MacDonald, Believer's Bible Commentary (1992)

16. BSF Notes Lesson 29 Revelation

17. https://www.churchofjesuschrist.org/study/manual/gospel-topics/race-and-the-priesthood?lang=eng

18. Conference Report October 1960, pp. 32-37

19. https://www.churchofjesuschrist.org/study/ensign/1985/01/joseph-smiths-recitals-of-the-first-vision?lang=eng

20. https://www.sunstonemagazine.com/passive-aggression-among-the-latter-day-saints-evidence-from-the-wasatch-front/

21. https://www.latimes.com/archives/la-xpm-2002-feb-20-mn-28924-story.html

22. https://archive.org/details/Ensign_Magazine-2005-04/page/n3/mode/2up

www.ingramcontent.com/pod-product-compliance
Lightning Source LLC
Chambersburg PA
CBHW031429120626
46545CB00006B/2325